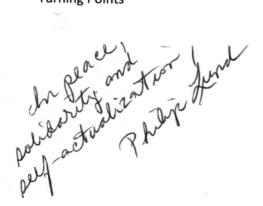

Turning Points

Discovering Meaning and Passion in Turbulent Times

Turning Points

TURNING POINTS

Discovering Meaning and Passion in Turbulent Times

Laurence Peters and

Jacqueline Mosio, Editors

ChangingTimesPress

This work is an anthology of essays by people who found their way
through turbulent times.

TURNING POINTS

Discovering Meaning and Passion in
Turbulent Times

Laurence Peters and

Jacqueline Mosio, Editors

ISBN 9781536825701

Cover art "The Memory Tree" by Christina Kieltyka

Cover design by Samantha Fernandez

To our readers who have met, are meeting,
or will meet their turning points.

Turning Points

"The opposite of love is not hate, it's indifference.
The opposite of art is not ugliness, it's indifference.
The opposite of faith is not heresy, it's indifference. And
the opposite of life is not death, it's indifference."
— Elie Wiesel (1928-2016)

Contents

Foreword   John Noltner
Introduction   Laurence Peters

Essays

William J. Anderson *Evolution of an Activist*	1
Burt Berlowe *If I Can Dream: From Mister Sandman to the King of Rock and Roll*	9
Robert J. Burrowes *Why Am I?*	26
Marianna Fransius *Making Peace Sexy*	36
Christina Kieltyka *Passion for the Beloved Earth*	40
Svetlana Kim *How I Survived in America with One Dollar and One Dream*	45
Amanda Lewis *Turning Points and Mrs. Dundee*	56
Juan Linares *Growing Dreams and Marketing Hope*	64
Philip Lund *A Persistent Echo*	71
Rose McGee *Sweet Potato Comfort Pie Power—Eyes On the Pie!*	81
Paul Mayer *A Monk in the Civil Rights Movement: Encounter with Dr. Martin Luther King, Jr.*	92
Michael Kiesow Moore *The End of War*	109
Jacqueline Mosio *Scenes from a Life*	115
Ray Myers *Changed During the Sixties*	127
Clem Nagel *You Had to Have Been There*	137
Elizabeth Nagel *When I Did the Math*	143
Robbie Orr *Three Days that Shook My World*	151
Laurence Peters *Belonging*	161
Roy Wolff *Be Calmed in Korea: The Making of a Peacemaker*	177
Lynne Zotalis *What Is Your Truth?*	189
Afterword Bao Phi, The Loft Literary Center	208
Acknowledgments	210

Foreword

We've been telling stories since before we had the written word. Stories pass on wisdom and share history. They help us understand ourselves and others, building relationships and breaking down barriers. Stories have the ability to expose universal truths in a way that simple facts and statistics cannot. If we choose to listen.

In this collection you will find stories transformative moments. Those ah-ha moments when we have a clarity of vision and purpose. Sometimes that clarity fades, but other times it redefines us and changes the course of our lives.

For me, it happened in my mid-twenties. My wife and I had just moved to a new city. We had a baby on the way and had joined a new church. I scheduled a meeting with Rick, the pastor, and explained to him that I had always wanted to be part of a church that had a global vision, a church that was involved with international aid work, whether it was educational, medical, or economic.

Rick listened intently and nodded up and down. He raised his eyebrows and smiled at all the right times and I thought I was getting through to him.

In my mind, I thought, "Yes! He is going to do this!"

When I was done talking, Rick sat back in his chair and thought for a moment. Then he looked me in the eye and said, "John, I think that's a great idea."

"Yes!" I thought again. But then Rick continued.

"Why don't you go ahead and make that happen, and I'll support you any way that I can."

The answer caught me off guard. I came looking for him to act and left with an invitation to take action myself. It was my own ah-ha moment. It was the moment I recognized that church...our community...and this world are nothing more than a bunch of people gathered together trying to understand what to do next and how to move forward. And if we see something that needs to be changed, then it's up to us to change it.

What is your clarion call? How has it changed your life? Perhaps you are still waiting to hear that sense of purpose and call to action. Sometimes it calls loudly, and sometimes it whispers. Make sure that you are listening.

John Noltner

John Noltner is an award-winning photographer and storyteller. Since 2009 he has crossed the country asking people the simple question, "What does peace mean to you?" Those stories are gathered in two books, **A Peace of My Mind: Exploring the Meaning of Peace One Story at a Time**, and **A Peace of My Mind: American Stories**. The stories are also produced as traveling exhibits that install across the country and are used to foster public dialog about conflict resolution, civic responsibility, and social change. His work can be found at www.apeaceofmymind.net.

Introduction

There are many reasons why people should tell their stories. We all know them and know that our stories have value to others. But we rationalize to ourselves about why we have not taken the time to write them down. Maybe we are not writers and don't think we have literary skill. Why bother, we ask ourselves, and who will read them anyway? We all have heard that voice in our head reciting some or all of these excuses. But there are other voices that are strongly calling us in a different direction. With many of us, the older we get, the more we realize the bitter truth that, for some of us all that will be left as our legacy are the words we leave behind.

This anthology of essays was put together because I read Burt Berlowe's excellent book, *The Compassionate Rebel Revolution: Ordinary People Changing the World,* and thought that the inspiring stories of over fifty advocates and activists who were brave and strong enough to challenge the received wisdom of their time to forge independent lives needed to be built upon. What Burt was writing about was an inspiring story of our era—but what about the rest of us who perhaps have not been consistent compassionate rebels, who may have wavered between the idealism of their youth and the need to get a job that could "put bread on the table"? What label could we use for these folks? Certainly they may not have seen their lives as in anyway heroic, but they were finding creative and interesting ways to advance their early idealism. While they were not fortunate enough to have their avocation fully become their vocation, as many of Burt's "compassionate rebels" had, they had at least preserved from their youth a tiny moment when they chose to become politically active or socially engaged with their communities.

So I called Burt after reading the book and we discussed some of these ideas, concluding that a large part of our baby boom generation might be up for documenting their lives as they reach the age where they are reflecting on the past and the legacy that they want to leave their children and grandchildren. Why not give this a go? Burt first wanted to try out the idea with his Peace and Social Justice Writers Group at The Loft in Minneapolis, Minnesota, and see what the reception might be. The group not only warmly embraced the idea, but through their networks put out a call for essays that would describe the critical turning points in people's lives and particular moments in their past where they became engaged with a set of people, events or ideas that changed them in some permanent way to become who they now are.

The challenge was to get as close as possible to the turbulent times we lived in and to see the choices as we saw them. Whether it involved the choice to evade the draft, or protest it, to travel, work on the farm or please our families by settling down in a regular career, we had to face, as Robert Louis Stevenson memorably remarked, "the banquet of consequences" that followed. The purpose in writing is not to record any heroism or saintliness but just to tell it like it was. To recount the way choices appeared to us—sometimes in dramatic ways and sometimes accidentally.

In one story Ray Myers, a Peace Corps volunteer, found himself in June 1968 "bouncing over and around potholes on a dusty dirt road in a jammed Indian public transit bus" and having a man next to him ask if he knew that Kennedy had been assassinated. "Yes, I did," replies Ray believing the man was referring to the death of President John Kennedy some years before in November 1963. Then he takes a look at the awful photograph displayed on the front page of the local newspaper: "the fallen Kennedy lying on the kitchen floor of the

Ambassador Hotel in Los Angeles." He realizes he must return home only to discover a land "more foreign to me than the streets of Dharwad, Karnataka." Moved by Kennedy's idealism, he takes a job teaching in inner city Philadelphia.

You can also take the case of Robbie Orr a few years later who also had lived in India and, upon reading another ghastly newspaper headline, felt "hot bolts of metal" shoot through him as he relaxed on a college lawn. The front page blasted out the news that "NIXON BOMBS HANOI in big bold 68-point type." The story went on to recount how the "Hanoi railway station, schools, hospitals and homes all swept away by a rolling wave of destruction as B-52s carpet bombed North Vietnam. Secretary of State Kissinger was quoted, "We have to force the Communists to negotiate seriously." Robbie describes the moment in exquisite detail when he decided that "a white skinny kid," who had so far only observed the sixties protests, had to do something as he walked across the campus and saw the students studying under trees like it was just another day and imagined "a wave of exploding earth swept across a field, engulfing a school. I could see B52s carpet bombing Grinnell; the Fine Arts Center exploded and a wave of destruction swallowed South Campus. I felt sick to my stomach and leaned against a tree." Robbie managed to mimeograph off "several hundred slightly smudged black and white leaflets" protesting the bombing and successfully organized 900 students in a sit-down hunger protest

In some ways, this book of essays can be regarded as a group portrait of a generation touched by the turbulent winds of midcentury America tossing many received values aside in their wake, and in so doing reshaping concepts of community and individual pathways forward. There seemed no safe or easy choices not just for men in terms of whether and how to avoid the draft but also for young women battling against gender stereotypes. Elizabeth Nagel's essay, for example, focuses on the challenge of how to reconcile motherhood with following a career. Many of the cultural voices of the time were telling her to stay home and she worked hard as a new mother to "make a fulfilling life for myself." But then one day when her two children grew out of infancy she "did the math. At mid-life, I would have no children to parent and a busy professional husband working long hours." It was a realization that shook her "to the core." Her journey was "to create a radically different life when my two children would be in grade school and gone for the day." As Elizabeth writes: "It was a huge step to take for a girl who had been programed to be an at-home wife and mother. Girl? I must have been at least thirty years old before I could think of myself as a woman."

Sometimes those life-changing decisions that occur during a moment of enlightenment do not end up with clear and happy closure. Lynne Zotalis and her husband Chuck adhered fiercely to Thoreau's admonition, "Go confidently in the direction of your dreams. Live the life you have imagined." Lynne documents so carefully both the joy and pain of living nine miles from the nearest grocery store and having to deal with disputed land rights. But the real strength of the piece is her battle to reflect on what she has learned from a difficult journey towards inner peace. She concluded that we either are diminished by our past or empowered by it. We clearly understand at the end of the essay that, despite the suffering she has had to endure that included the tragic freak death of her husband, writing about her life has helped her see the experiences as empowering. Rather than being trapped by the past, she is now turning her attention to a new future.

All of these essays are touched with idealism that was characteristic of the period and is so sorely absent in many areas today. It was the dreams of the '60s that propelled Burt Berlowe to understand how to combine his writing with political activism. To illustrate the power of the change, Burt masterfully takes us through the way the lyrics of the 1950s were full of another kind of dreaming about a culture of contentment that was fulfilling individual needs and wishes but was in the end pleasantly vacuous. The essay's genius is that Burt allows us to discover for ourselves how the new sixties dreams first emerged for him, not emanating from the TV or radio but from the streets. Burt precisely locates the time and place in 1969 when his new view of the American dream began after hearing about a planned antiwar demonstration in New York and deciding to take the Greyhound bus with his wife to New York to make his voice heard. Burt helps us to understand the mood that first grabbed him as he tells the story of how "The street was filled for miles on end with all kinds of people: young and old, black and white, pastors and teachers and students and laborers and housewives, men and women pushing baby strollers or carrying children on their backs—the peacemakers of the future getting their first taste of public protest. Although we didn't all know each other personally, there was a camaraderie brought on by the shared feelings and emotions and commitment of that day. I felt no longer alone but rather part of a larger movement. I could not be sure if or when the war would end. But for the first time since it began, I personally felt the political winds shifting." He helps us realize how all of this must have felt even extending to the details of the ride back home where he began a journal and later a short story about the fateful day.

But for many, the idealistic vision of those times has been hard to sustain. Jacqueline Mosio worked as an editor with the tireless priest activist Paul Mayer who, among his many projects and efforts, co-founded Children of War that brought together young people from conflict areas around the world for healing and to reach out to peers in the U.S. through speaking tours. She asks the question we all might have of someone so committed: "How did he do it? What motivated him and kept his hopes and spirit burning bright?" Mayer's account of the moment that propelled him irrevocably forward into a life of activism is also recounted here.

It is clear as the 20th century recedes into history that more than ever we need these stories of people at the passion-filled turning points in their lives. Historians looking back on this period will have many accounts of the way leaders like a Betty Friedan or a Tom Hayden made their decisions to move in one direction or another, but not as much about those who escaped the spotlight chose to live out their lives.

We hope you enjoy reading these candid portraits of people trying to come to terms and make peace with their past selves and find the sources of pride and idealistic energy that they continue to nurture. We look forward to your comments. Please do get in touch with us if you would like to share your story of how you found your pivot moments. We would like to continue to publish these volumes if there is enough interest. We see it as a documentary group portrait of a generation still in motion, still interested in working to make the planet a more peaceful fair and equal place for all our children to grow up in.

Laurence Peters
January 2016

ESSAYS

Turning Points

William J. Anderson

Evolution of an Activist

During my K-12 years in Anoka, Minnesota, education in American history focused on the settlement of North America and the birth of the United States. Life, liberty and the pursuit of happiness made perfect sense. So did religious freedom and no taxation without representation.

But when slavery entered the discussion and had been considered an acceptable way of life during the colonial period, I immediately thought it was wrong. I didn't understand how a country based on liberty and freedom could allow the enslavement and exploitation of another person. And yet, the United States had allowed it from the start.

Already, the contradictory nature of human behavior was leaving me perplexed.

*

The CBS Evening News with Walter Cronkite came on at 5:30, Monday through Friday. I was eleven or so and the Vietnam War was raging. About the time I came in for dinner, he would be reciting the score for the week: The number of American, ARVN (South Vietnamese), North Vietnamese and Viet Cong soldiers killed and injured in combat. The numbers were too large, but my young mind took some comfort when I saw our losses were smaller than those of the other armies.

It didn't take long—too many images of Buddhist monks committing self-immolation, girls running from Napalm attacks, prisoners being executed on the street—and I was questioning the value and sanity of our war efforts. No comfort could be derived from the numbers.

Later I would hear stories about friendly fire, officers getting fragged (killed by their own troops), Hamburger Hill and massacres like the one in My Lai, continue to watch the weekly scores climb, and begin to wonder about the effectiveness of our leadership and the purpose of our mission.

*

The things the people asked for during the Civil Rights movement seemed perfectly reasonable and completely understandable, once I got past the fact that what they were asking for should have already been theirs. After all, this was America and we'd been around for more than 180 years. And slavery had already been abolished for a century.

I watched the stories about the marches and felt that Right was being proven by the non-violent natures of the activists. And when they were met with violence and didn't respond in kind, it enhanced the image that the activists were on the correct path, the high road.

After a while, I heard stories about separate entrances and drinking fountains, the Freedom Riders, lynchings, church bombings and murders and was appalled that a progressive and knowledgeable nation could be so entrenched in hate and ignorance. Again, it all went against what our country had been based on since its birth. Especially since I had such a difficult time seeing the differences in people—to me we were all human and all animals. It would be like hating a chameleon when he blended in to the brown couch but loving him when he blended in with the green curtains. It's the same chameleon. Deep down, we're all the same animal, too.

*

As a product of the television generation, I grew up watching shows like *Gunsmoke, Bonanza, Combat* and the war and western movies that played every Saturday. I learned that you're not supposed to like your enemies. At some point, I realized that the people fighting the wars are not the people living near the wars, that the people in war zones are victims of war as much as the people who die in combat. And I figured out that the odds are excellent that none of those victims were actually responsible for the war.

I learned about enough broken treaties and mistreatment of indigenous and civilian populations that I found my allegiances shifting. Movies such as *Little Big Man* and *Billy Jack* and the events that took place at Pine Ridge and Wounded Knee again had me questioning the behavior of our civilization. As did the genocides that keep happening around the world, the ones that we seem to not notice until the number of dead is in the six figures. Oppression and extermination are not acceptable.

But neither is ignoring reality in the hope that it will go away. Pine Ridge County, the poorest county in the richest country, lost its water system because of an ice storm at about the same time Haiti had its earthquake. We sent aid and ran a benefit concert for Haiti. But the lack of water in Pine Ridge County barely received a mention in the national press. I never heard if we made any extra efforts to correct the situation or not, or even how long they didn't have water. I couldn't help but wonder why our focus was so narrow that we could only see one circumstance of suffering at a time. And why our attention span was so short that by the end of the concert, we didn't hear much about either place. Are the lives of the people of Haiti so much better from one day of music and fundraising that we can already move on?

*

The death of Dr. Martin Luther King, Jr. was a tragic loss. But I believed that someone would step up and lead in his place and that the movement would continue. When the riots began, I thought, "Oh, don't do that," because I believed it would be counterproductive to the effort and not at all how Dr. King would have wanted everyone to behave.

Two months later, when Bobby Kennedy was killed, I thought we lost another voice of reason. And I wondered what people were so afraid of that they had to kill the messengers of peace.

*

The kids in my Anoka neighborhood spent a lot of time playing at a park and in a small section of woods at the end of Elm Street. Once, we used a Mason jar of drinking water we carried to put out a fire a different group of kids had started. But most of the time we just did kid stuff.

One day, we saw how much litter had collected along the edge of the woods. A group of us decided we should clean our park. This was years before somebody developed the Adopt-a-Park program. I know Dan, Tom and Chuck were with me, but there were probably others too. We picked up everything we could and packaged it for disposal. I'm not sure whose garbage cans we filled or if what we collected was too much for pickup and had to be hauled to the dump.

People from the nearby apartments came and asked us what we were doing. They wanted to know who was making us pick up the litter. We told them it was our idea, that it just needed doing. They all went away smiling, telling us it was a great idea. One lady brought us cookies and soft drinks and insisted we take a break and enjoy them, which we did. But restoring our park, and knowing the idea was a good one and was appreciated was what made the effort worthwhile.

*

Before the advent of the *Animal Planet*, Jack Hanna and Steve Irwin, my sixth-grade classmates selected me as the likely replacement for Marlin Perkins on Mutual of Omaha's *Wild Kingdom*. I was a lover of everything crawly. And of all of the animals that weren't crawly, too. When it was announced that Minnesota needed a new zoo and they were asking the kids to become members, I got my parents to send in my dollar. I received my sticker and certificate saying I was a member.

Something convinced me, however, that animals needed to be protected but wild. Maybe it was the death of a couple of pets—things that shouldn't have been pets in the first place. Or maybe it was looking in the eyes of the apes at Como Zoo in their glass habitat, or the dolphins at the Minnesota Zoo as they swam circles in their undersized tank and looked into the face of everyone leaning over the railing. I felt a connection to the souls inside.

Humans need to see the other inhabitants of our planet to help understand our place in a larger system, and zoos may be the last refuge for some animals, so I support their existence and their efforts. But I feel guilty walking free among the animal residents of the zoo and I grow depressed if I think about it for too long.

Now, when a bird finds its way into the garage or a bee into the house, my family and I go to great lengths to get the animals back outside where they belong. We recently did it with a couple of rodents that came in an open egress window. We've stopped in the middle of county roads and scooped up turtles and driven them to a safer location. We brake for squirrels, frogs and toads. Except for mosquitoes and wood ticks, all of those small lives have value and I regret the unnecessary loss of every one of them.

But I also recognize the need for balance. One of the ways nature maintains balance is with predation. If we eliminate too many predators, nature introduces disease to help find balance.

As humans spread and force out the predators but feed the cute ones that visit our backyards, we see the rise of things like Chronic Wasting Disease or Bird Flu and have to wonder if it will stay contained within a single species. Or we see so many accidents between cars and deer that the freeways are littered with corpses of Bambi, his family and friends. And as we continue to indiscriminately consume resources and spread at an alarming rate, I wonder what might be coming our way to help us achieve balance.

*

Patriotic fervor was inescapable after the attacks of September 11, 2001. My hope was that we would respond with caution. We had the support of the world but memory is short-lived, and too often derived from polls, which means such support is as fleeting as the wind. I was afraid that if we were not careful, we would lose the support of even our closest friends and could make things worse, that world peace would become even more tenuous.

*

Afghanistan presented a different set of concerns. Had we learned nothing from our time in Vietnam? Or from the Soviet attempts to tame Afghanistan? Did we even need to be there? Would our presence actually change things for the better in the long-term?

*

If victory in these conflicts had been attained without the loss of a single American soldier, how come our people started dying afterwards? If our mission was accomplished, as we were told, why did so many have to die? And why do they continue to do so? Were we really prepared to care for those who came home, injured or not? Why is the suicide rate among people who saw combat so high? Shouldn't we be seeking the answers to questions such as these before we commit another person to a conflict with questionable motivations?

*

My life as an activist has been tempered by responsibility. I have worked hard to take care of my family, and my own little world that I actually had very little control over, and worked too many hours. As a result, I never made it to a protest, participated in a rally or a march.

But I drove the companies where I worked long and hard to reduce, reuse and recycle, insisted we be good corporate citizens and tried to always do the right thing just because it was the right thing to do.

I voted. Participation in the system is essential if you wish to bitch.

And I wrote. I have plenty of material regarding war, social justice and environmental responsibility. But I have slacked in the marketing and distribution.

Recognizing that my writing might be my most effective tool, and wanting to improve as a writer and as an activist, I became a member of the Peace and Social Justice Writing Group at the Loft Literary Center. Surrounded by people who write extensively on the subject and have participated in rallies, been arrested and marched with Dr. King, I found a place to belong and learn and to draw inspiration.

I recognize and admit that my efforts as an activist and writer have been not been as visible as the work of some of my compatriots. Nor has it been as extensive or productive as I would have wished. My approach has been scattered, torn in too many directions, as I see too many issues to be able to focus on just one aspect of life on Earth. So in spite of my evolution as a human being, my concern for the planet and all of its inhabitants, I don't feel as if I've done enough to leave a better world for my daughters. I look at the efforts of other activists, find joy in their efforts and accomplishments and wish I could have been at their sides.

I understand, however, that the impact one person has is difficult to measure. Incremental change of any type is hard to recognize. Kind of like waking up one morning and seeing a head full of gray hair—you wonder when it happened but everybody around you saw it progress gradually, one hair at a time. You're just too close. So maybe the world isn't visibly better as I leave it for my daughters, but maybe I taught them the tools they need to continue to improve it.

And with the birth of my granddaughter Betsy on March 19, 2012, I realize I still have a responsibility and an opportunity to try. I play with her or watch her as she sleeps and have to believe there is still enough time left to leave her with a better world. If nothing else, maybe I can show her that it is worth the effort to keep trying.

William J. Anderson is a husband, father, grandfather, poet, writer, questioner of all things, devoted listener and enlightened optimist living in Champlin, Minnesota. Bill is a member of the Peace and Social Justice Writing Group at The Loft Literary Center, the Wordwhippers critique group and the Lead Us Write writing group. Someday soon you'll be able to find more samples of his writing at his website **wmjanderson.com**.

Burt Berlowe

If I Can Dream: From Mister Sandman

to the King of Rock and Roll

"'Music is the soundtrack of our lives'. If you step away and view your life as a movie, this quote from [American Bandstand Producer] Dick Clark rings so true. A certain song can bring back a person, place or event in a second."
— Ann Roberts Talbot, writer for the Melrose Mirror.

It's the fading moments of the last day of 2014 and I am performing an annual ritual of watching late night television as the masses of people line up for miles along Broadway and come together for Dick Clark's "Rockin' Eve" in New York City's Times Square. Once again, it's time to bid adieu to the old year and to welcome in the new one as the giant ball drops at midnight, followed by a soundtrack of "Auld Lang Syne," Frank Sinatra's tribute to Manhattan, and live performances by current musical superstars. The traditional celebration marks another juncture on the American calendar and an occasion for personal reflection on the past year and it's half-century rendezvous with a long ago yesterday when transformative events in Times Square and beyond became critical turning points for America and for my evolution into changing times.

Verse One: All I Have To Do Is Dream

"Yesterday when I was young the thousand dreams I dreamed, the splendid things I planned I'd always built to last on weak and shifting sand. Yesterday when I was young So many happy songs were waiting to be sung."
— "Yesterday When I Was Young" by Roy Clark

Yesterday when I was very young there were so many songs waiting to be sung. Dream songs and dreamy doo wop ballads rolled off of Wurlitzer juke boxes, car and home radios, drive-in movie speakers and rpm record turntables, especially made for slow dancing, making out with your teenage crush or to listen to alone in dreamy moments. It may have all begun with "Mister Sandman," that catchy little doo wop ballad released in 1954 by the Chordettes who harmoniously play a lonely, love-starved woman begging the mythical snooze-inducing character to bring her the man of her dreams. The Sandman made a return visit in 1958 when Roy Orbison recorded "In Dreams," where he talks about "a candy-colored clown they call the sandman tiptoes to my room every night just to sprinkle stardust and to whisper...everything is all right. In dreams I walk with you. In dreams I talk to you. In dreams your mine all the time. We're together in dreams."

There was a proliferation of dream songs during the 1950s, simple, singable ballads that were mainly about romantic yearning for that special someone who has not yet come along or isn't present at the moment, wishful thinking and a fantasy substitute for what was missing in real time. For my former self growing up in that decade, the dream songs had some special meanings. Two of them: The Everly Brothers "All I Have to do is Dream" and Bobby Darin's "Dream Lover" became the soundtracks of my first two dating relationships. "All I Have to do is Dream" spoke of the wishful longing: "Whenever I want you all I have to is dream…" and of the angst: "Only trouble is, gee whiz, I'm dreaming my life away." Dream Lover was a plea for romantic companionship "So I don't have to dream alone." I would play and sing those songs over and over again while we were together and then through tears when the break-up came.

Gradually, the music of that time became a symphonic soundtrack for an unfolding biopic of an adolescent venture into an emerging new culture. I became a fan of shows like *American Bandstand* on TV and the top 40 stations on the radio, with a personal collection of singles and albums to spin on my record player. I formed and promoted rock bands and individual performers, and composed my own songs with just a few chords on a cheap guitar, some of which were recorded and played on local radio stations, and, for a while, fostered dreams of being a successful songwriter until the reality of that challenge set in.

My first encounter with the future king of rock and roll came in the mid-1950s. I was standing near a concession stand across the street from my high school where popular songs of the day were blaring from a radio. I stopped to listen to the guttural, echoing voice of an emerging new singer the announcer identified as Elvis Presley singing about a place where lonely people with unfulfilled dreams "gather in the gloom." I thought it was the voice of a Black man. Little did I know that a king was emerging and that I would be one of his most loyal subjects.

When Elvis burst onto the scene with his unique sound and provocative moves, the music that followed became a powerful indication that the dreamy innocence of the '50s couldn't last. Rock 'n' roll would be the message that would shake the underpinnings of society and signal a new revolution of dramatic changes in our politics, our culture and our way of life.

Life in the 1950s was often depicted and celebrated in song. The music reflected a culture focused on fulfilling individual needs and wishes. It was the decade of the American Dream, a relatively innocent, civil and prosperous time with an emphasis on family values, upward mobility, status and conformity.

The U.S. was swept up in a wave of unparalleled affluence featuring the longest economic boom in history, fueled by the impact of post-war baby boomers with the education and financial resources to dream of great expectations for themselves and their loved ones. It was a time of rising affluence and cheap prices—of five-cent candy bars, dollar-a-gallon gasoline and dollar matinee movies. The average cost of owning a cookie-cutter home was $12,650; of a new car, $3,233. A loaf of bread cost 22 cents. In a nation of fewer than 50 million families, almost 60 million automobiles were registered. Most Americans could push a button to watch their favorite sitcom about the ideal nuclear family, listen to a favorite song on the Victrola, and use an arsenal of handy electrical appliances.

A sense of hope and optimism prevailed for those striving for the middle-class—the feeling that there were no limits to how comfortable and happy Americans could be. There was a widespread assumption that America was a land of opportunity, a just, democratic and free society whose only problems were caused by outside agitators. But under the radar the rumblings of social change were about to explode, rocking the world for decades to come. In cities everywhere, in pockets of poverty and oppression, there were many who did not share in the American Dream and had little hope of achieving it, whose lives were not being played out in TV sitcoms, movie dramas, hit songs, political rhetoric or in the average mindset of the times.

As the '60s unfolded, many Americans began to take a critical look at the contradictions in their society. They still believed that their country could work for everyone who was willing to pull themselves up by their bootstraps, but they also increasingly recognized the growing poverty amidst middle-class affluence, the bitter racism in some parts of the country, the lack of equal opportunity.

Behind the scenes the stage was being set for the commencement of a new era of political and social change—a harsher, disruptive time propelled by the young, the disenchanted and those with a social conscience. An emerging counterculture movement began to resist materialism and conformity and seek alternative ways to live and to create a more ideal world for everyone.

Author James Farber has referred to the '60s as "The Age of Great Dreams." In his book of that name he says, "In the 1960s Americans dared to chance grand dreams." The '60s insurgency was driven by the explosion of rock and folk/protest music that fed the seeds of an emerging rebellion against the status quo and for political and social change.

A climactic point in this music revolution occurred in the summer of 1963 when some 400,000 people gathered at an historic Newport, Rhode Island folk festival to watch rising young musicians, including an emerging Bob Dylan, playing acoustic instruments and singing gospel ballads, blues and, most of all, new protest music. The Newport folk festival marked a significant turning point in popular music and culture. By the end of that decade, folk music and a spin-off folk rock were absorbed into the mainstream

With the blossoming of the new decade, the nature of dream songs began to change. A previously little-known song became a protest anthem "Last night I had the strangest dream I've never had before. I dreamt that the world had put an end to war." Beatle John Lennon's "Imagine" took the concept further asking people to join together to envision a more peaceful and civil society. "This is the dawning of the Age of Aquarius" celebrated the perceived fulfillment of a counterculture dream.

Elvis, whose early hit "Love Me Tender" talked about personal dreams fulfilled, was realizing his own dream of becoming a movie star. In 1962, he released a song from a movie of the same name that urged people to "Follow that dream wherever it happens to lead you."

It was a watershed decade when people followed their dreams into challenging new places, when the perception and nature of the American Dream changed dramatically from the isolated self-centered yearnings that focused on individual welfare, societal ambition and conformity, into an emerging new reality that would expand the nature of dreams and visions beyond the parochial and personal to encompass the common good, a concerned view of the state of humanity and what could be done about it—a new journey into previously unknown places and bigger dreams with unpredictable and challenging outcomes.

My former self grew up on the edges of the American dream, raised in the growing Wild West town of Tucson, Arizona, in a modest single family home on a quiet residential street nestled between palm trees, mesquite bushes and the canyon of mountains surrounding the city. Like so many others, we were a comfortable nuclear family like you watched on shows like *Father Knows Best, The Brady Bunch* and *Ozzie and Harriet.*

My politically liberal, middle-class parents had no higher aspirations. They taught me about compassion for the less fortunate and the capacity of the federal government to make a difference in people's lives. At the same time, I was caught up in my own personal dreams. I still have vivid memories of my father, often dressed in an undershirt and khaki pants, seated at a wooden desk punching the large lettered keys of a manual black L.C Smith typewriter to create the next edition of a postal union newsletter. In a profound way, he was trying to reinvent his American dream: a promising journalism career derailed by health problems that forced the family to migrate out of the cold Minnesota climate to the warmer weather in a town known for its medicinal benefits as well as for its burgeoning tourist industry. Unable to work in his chosen profession, he was employed at the local post office while pursuing a passion for writing and politics. He edited a union newsletter, spent hours perusing local newspapers for items he could respond to in letters to the editor, wrote scathing commentary, and worked on political campaigns, pausing frequently to let my caregiver mother administer cortisone shots to stop his asthma attacks.

While he had progressive political views, he clung to some old-fashioned values. On our frequent walks around the neighborhood, he would express his discomfort with my rebellious tendencies—the Elvis sideburns, the immersion in rock music and seeming resistance of authority. We would also talk about how he wasn't able to become the journalist he wanted to be and how I could achieve the dream of a journalistic career that had eluded him.

Verse Two: I Have a Dream

Through the early to middle years of the '60s, my dreams and the urge to fulfill them remained mostly personal, preoccupied with college graduation, a move back to Minneapolis, newspaper reporting jobs and a romantic relationship with a music major from a tiny rural Minnesota town. I was becoming aware of and angry about the violence and injustices that seemed to be all around me and had a growing empathy and admiration for the emerging resistance movements and the iconic figures who were urging us to have a new vision of the American Dream. I began to harbor dreams of being a reporter who would cover the major political and social issues of the day.

I was inspired by the words and promise of President Kennedy the first time I heard him over a loudspeaker blaring across my college campus. Years later, I would especially recall a quote from a speech he gave to a labor union crowd a year before his assassination and that his brother Bobby would repeat in his aborted 1968 presidential campaign: "Some folks see things as they are and ask why. I dream of things that never were and ask why not." I had watched the TV coverage of Martin Luther King's "I have a dream" speech at the momentous march on Washington in the summer of 1963 when the dreamers came by the multitudes from around the country chanting and singing, crying out for the freedom and justice, weary from the riding and walking that day and from the burdens that weighed them down and deferred their dreams, clinging to each other, coming to this place in search of hope. In a dramatic, poetic syntax that echoed across the D.C. Mall and the American landscape, Dr. King talked about a dream he had where "one day little black boys and black girls will be able to join hands with little white boys and white girls as sisters and brothers…where people will be judged not by the color of their skin but by the content of their character." It was, he said, part of the American dream. Actually, it changed the definition of the American dream. No longer did people merely imagine a better life for themselves and others. They took action to make it happen.

"There's something happening here/ What it is ain't exactly clear/ There's a man with gun over there saying people you better beware /…hey there, what's that sound/ Everybody look what's going down."
— "Something's Happening Here" by Buffalo Springfield

Like so many Americans, I can clearly remember where I was on that tragic November day in 1963. It began as just another day in the compact office of the Yuma, Arizona *Daily Sun*, the main newspaper of this hot and dusty western town. A small group of us reporters were pounding away at our manual typewriters, gathering story information on dial telephones, and periodically checking the news wire telegraph machine and the stacks of regular mail piled on desks waiting to be opened, when we were jolted by the loud but somber male voice blaring from a portable radio in the next room, announcing the assassination of President Kennedy. I had gotten up from my desk to cut some paper at the nearby paper cutting machine. When I heard the news my body jolted and a chill raced down my spine. The cutter blade came down almost chopping off a front finger. I had narrowly avoided a physical wound but the emotional scars I experienced along with much of America would stay for a long time, fueling my anger at the violence in society and how it could bring a whole world to its knees. But even as this seminal decade was unfolding before me, I didn't immediately grasp it. I had left adolescent angst behind but was unsure of what would lie ahead. My pursuit of a journalism career began in Arizona but later took me back to Minnesota and a challenging world of professional pursuits and romantic relationships. For several years in the mid-60s I didn't fully acknowledge the restlessness and searching that was stirring inside waiting to emerge and be part of larger dreams.

Verse 3: If I Can Dream

"There must be lights burning brighter somewhere/ Got to be birds flying higher in a sky so blue/ If I can dream of a better land/ Where all my brothers walk hand in hand/ Tell me why, oh why oh why can't my dream come true."
— "If I Can Dream" by Elvis Presley

The events of 1968 shook the world around me—the assassinations of Dr. King and Bobby Kennedy, the turbulent civil rights protests, the riots at the democratic national convention, the continuing war abroad and the growing movement to end it. I began to search for ways to become actively involved in the movement for peace and justice. Gradually, my dreams would become less centered around personal gratification and more about imagining a better world for all of humankind.

Then as 1968 was coming to an end, I was inspired by a song Elvis Presley sang at his comeback concert called "If I Can Dream." It seemed to take up the theme of Dr. King's speech and to represent the new American dream. A year later, Elvis would record another song with a strong social message: the emotionally profound "In the Ghetto." The king of rock and roll had evolved with the culture that adored and sometimes vilified him. He was no longer just a revolutionary rock icon, who was rejuvenating a popularity that had been diminished by the passage of time and the arrival of the musical British Invasion in the U.S. He had become a dreamer of social change.

"We're lost in a cloud/ With too much rain/ We're trapped in a world/ that's troubled with pain/But as long as a man has the strength to dream...he can fly."

In 1969, America fulfilled a dream of landing on the moon and thousands of rebellious youth dreamed of love and peace as they flocked to Woodstock in rural New York in mid-August for a revolutionary three-day festival of sex, drugs and rock and roll that would become an iconic moment for the '60s counterculture—a massive rebellion against the mores of American society, an apparent climax to a decade of disruption and dissent. On October 15 of that year the dreams turned to action on the streets of several American cities. Ten million people came together to demonstrate against the lingering Vietnam War. I was working at a newspaper in a Minneapolis suburb when I heard about the planned New York City demonstration. My wife and I rode a greyhound bus to New York, stayed overnight in a church chapel with pews for beds, and joined the march the following day amidst the ranks of countless dreamers, movers and shakers.

It was an overcast, drizzly day, as we walked through the midst of downtown Manhattan, between towering buildings and small shops with bars on their windows and scores of police officers lined up like palace guards, hands crossed, billy clubs at their sides, faces grim and unmoving, watching and waiting for trouble to happen. It never did.

The march proceeded down Broadway past the famous Central Park with its 68 miles of paths, roads and bridges attracting a cross-section of American diversity by the millions each year. This section of lower Broadway is the historical location for the city's ticker-tape parades, and is sometimes called the Canyon of Heroes. Now, a far different kind of parade was taking place led by a new breed of heroes.

I walked amidst groups of people in front and behind and alongside as the soundtrack of singing and chanting of antiwar songs and slogans echoed through the misty air. The street was filled for miles on end with all kinds of people: young and old, black and white, pastors and teachers and students and laborers and housewives, men and women pushing baby strollers or carrying children on their backs—the peacemakers of the future getting their first taste of public protest. Although we didn't all know each other personally, there was a camaraderie brought on by the shared feelings and emotions and commitment of that day. I felt no longer alone but rather part of a larger movement. I could not be sure if or when the war would end. But for the first time since it began, I personally felt the political winds shifting

Then, suddenly the thunderous soundtrack of dissent was bathed in multicolored flashing lights as the march ended in the neon canyon famously known as a crossroads of the world and the center of the universe, a famous entertainment hub known for group celebration. Times Square had suddenly become a focal point of the largest public protest ever held in the United States, a coming together of a movement that would eventually play a role in bringing the war to an end. The famous square where thousands gather every New Year's Eve to sing Auld Lang Synge was now witness to the turning of a new page of history.

On the ride back home I began to journal that transformative experience as well as observations of a young hippie couple who were making their own version of the American flag in the seat behind me. I later wrote a story about that day in New York City setting in motion a lasting connection between my writing and activism that would continue in the decades to come.

The walk that began for me in downtown Manhattan gradually accelerated into a long-distance marathon with twists and turns and detours along the way. The tumultuous '60s gave way to a challenging new decade. I left behind the early days of rock and roll, a suburban apartment, my last mainstream newspaper job and a failed marriage and began a search for a new direction. It would eventually lead to a rendezvous with another Central Park and the downtown of a major urban metropolis.

In the mid-1970s, I moved to the Loring Park neighborhood in Minneapolis, with its rows of walk-up apartment buildings and its calm, scenic park. Formerly called Central Park more than a century ago, Loring Park, on the edge of downtown Minneapolis, is the namesake of its surrounding residential community. Its shimmering twin pond reflects images of the downtown and neighborhood skyline as a stark reminder of how they all relate to each other. It became for me a refreshing retreat from the rigors of those trying times and a place to reflect on the past and dream new dreams, while realizing that it would take more than dreaming life away to make change happen. In the process, my metamorphosis into a new current self would be complete as my writing and activism would again come together. I joined the Loring neighborhood organization's futile efforts to save their community from encroaching expansion of downtown urban renewal and gentrification, edited the neighborhood newspaper and published a history book commemorating the centennial of the park. I also worked as a community organizer for a coalition of central city neighborhoods, published articles and essays on downtown life and development and a book featuring the stories of activists in those communities. In the process, I found a new passion: the Twin Cities neighborhood movement.

Years later, I would join peace and justice organizations, attend marches and demonstrations, and promote the efforts of others who were genuinely working towards a non-violent world, eventually leading to the publication of books on peaceful parenting and the two-volume series of stories of compassionate rebels—everyday heroes who cared about an issue or cause and acted upon it in ways that bucked the status quo and led to peaceful, positive change. In the process, I increasingly realized the value of the previously untold stories of ordinary people who can and do change the world and can inspire others to move from thought and concern to action. Those of us who came of age in the '60s stood on the shoulders of peacemaker heroes and compassionate rebels we admired. Nowadays, when I am no longer young, my focus, along with other veteran activists, is to offer our weary shoulders to budding peace builders and compassionate rebels and to serve as role models and mentors for those who will be carrying on the movement for a better world.

Verse Four: Keep right on dreamin'

"....I'll Keep on dreamin'/ Keep right on dreamin' / Dreamin' till my dreams come true."
— "Dreamin'" by Johnny Burnette

Do we dare to dream again?

As longtime political prisoner Mumia Abu Jamal writes: "The music arises from a generation that feels, with some justice, that they have been betrayed by those who have come before them. That they are, at best, tolerated in schools, feared on the streets, and almost inevitably destined for the hell holes of prison. Once again, our country is at a turning point in its evolution as a democratic society, where the notion of the American dream is being challenged and redefined. With all of the gains of the civil rights movement and the election of a black president, African-Americans remain the victims of disproportionate incarceration and law enforcement profiling.

A recent survey shows the largest income gap between rich and poor in the nation's history. Another reports that 64 percent of the U.S. citizenry no longer believes in or identifies with the mainstream concept of the American Dream and 57 percent say that race relations in the U.S. are bad. The response has been a new civil rights movement that hopefully will take America and the world into a new era where as Dr. King said "the arc is long but it bends toward justice."

In the last few months of 2014 profound déjà vu moments took place on the streets of urban America. Once again the chants and songs for civil rights rose up on the site of the 1963 Washington D.C. march, and the 1969 demonstration in New York City, and in some 50 cities across the country, disrupting freeway traffic, Christmas shoppers, and the apathy of urban America.

Evoking memories of civil rights demonstrations of past decades, protestors flocked to rallies in response to the police shootings of young unarmed black men in Ferguson, Missouri, Staten Island and in other communities around the nation. The soundtrack of freedom songs and accompanying chants rang out: "Black lives Matter." "No Justice No Peace." "Hands Up. Don't Shoot." A teacher held up a sign that said her black students still have dreams. Another sign read "Here come the dreamers" as protesters claimed to be changing history.

On December 14, 2014 more than 25,000 people stretching for at least 20 blocks marched through lower Manhattan and across the Brooklyn Bridge pushing children in strollers, waving black liberation flags and carrying signs, ending up at police headquarters. Similar gatherings were held into the next month and on Dr. King's birthday in front of the U.S. capitol, on the steps of the Boston statehouse, in the streets of San Francisco, at a King statue at the University of Texas, at the Mall of America in Minneapolis and throughout the country.

These followed on the heels of huge climate change rallies in September in New York City, Minneapolis, and even as far away as London, where one of the organizers called it "the greatest grassroots movement of all time," and previous demonstrations by the new dreamers for immigration reform, economic justice, and others demanding equity and equality.

As the anniversary of the historic march on Selma, Alabama approached, a new movie about that historic event was released to critical acclaim. And on the day we celebrate the birthday of Martin Luther King, actors from the movie, along with major supporter Oprah Winfrey led a re-enactment of the Selma march over the Pettis Bridge. They were joined by Congressman John Lewis, who was badly beaten on the bridge during the original Selma protest. This powerful new movement reminds me of yesterday when I was young, when ordinary people changed the concept of the American Dream and turned society on its head, when the dreams constantly changed to fit the times and become reservoirs of hope for a better world.

The music and the culture have changed dramatically over time. The dreams of the counterculture revolution never fully reached fruition. The dreamy doo wop songs went the way of drive-in theaters, high school sock hops, dial phones and manual typewriters. The fervent, impassioned rebellion of the '60s became, for a long while, a seemingly distant echo reverberating through the annals of the past. The great dreamers who led the way through our most tumultuous times would fade into history, leaving a legacy that would defy the test of time.

And the beat goes on in the classic songs that we continue to sing, the ringing words and historic actions of the new generation of dreamers that have inspired so many to carry on and start anew, to dream their own dreams and play their own kind of music.

Nowadays, long after the yesterday when I was young, my mental jukebox is constantly full, spinning all kinds of oldies but goodies, tunes and lyrics I can recall as if I just heard them, songs waiting impatiently to be sung over and over again just as they were when they were the soundtrack of the most transformative era in American history. And, one song, in particular, remains an inspirational anthem:

"There must be peace and understanding sometime/ Strong winds of promise that will blow away/ All the doubt and fear/ If I can dream of a warmer sun/ Where hope keeps shining on everyone... " — "If I Can Dream" by Elvis Presley

We've come a long way since the visit from Mister Sandman.

Burt Berlowe is an award-winning author and journalist who specializes in writing and publishing the stories of ordinary people involved in positive social change. His publication of two books of inspiring compassionate rebel stories and his contribution to this anthology mark the culmination of a long and eventful turning point journey through turbulent times that has led to an intersection of two passions: writing and activism.

Along the way he has been constantly inspired by the insights and experiences gained during that journey, learning from the lessons and accomplishments, and the unfulfilled hopes and dreams of the 1960s and beyond. Through personal observation and direct involvement in transformative social movements and advocacy journalism, he has been impressed with and reported on the extraordinary efforts of average citizens to challenge the status quo and make the world a better place for current and future generations, and by the power of storytelling to make that happen.

During the '70s and '80s he published books and articles on the history of social change in Minneapolis central city neighborhoods while working as a community organizer and journalist in those communities and co-authored three books on peaceful parenting while involved in efforts to reduce family violence. More recently, he has become increasingly concerned about the ongoing focus on violence and repression in our culture and the need to tell the underreported stories of everyday heroes who are working to promote a more peaceful and just society.

This led to a significant turning point: the publication of two anthologies of those stories: *The Compassionate Rebel: Energized by*

Anger, Motivated by Love, and *The Compassionate Rebel Revolution: Ordinary People Changing the World*, now accompanied by an educator's guide for classroom use, a music CD and a dozen video interviews, all designed to use storytelling as a tool for building the next generation of compassionate rebels.

In recent months, Berlowe has joined the growing ranks of peace journalists who are working to change the stories that are featured in the media and in our culture. That has included contributing articles linking compassionate rebellion and peace journalism to national peace and justice organizations and scholarly publications, including *The Peace Journalist,* the *Journal of Peace Studies*, the Peace Alliance, Waging Nonviolence and the Alliance for Peacebuilding while remaining active in the Loft Peace and Social Justice Writers group and the Minnesota Alliance of Peacemakers. He is also contributing to the publication of a book on the history of his Seward neighborhood, including a chapter on social activism.

Robert J. Burrowes

Why am I?

July 1, 1942: The unescorted and unmarked Japanese prisoner-of-war ship *Montevideo Maru* was torpedoed off Luzon by the submarine *USS Sturgeon*. The *Montevideo Maru* sank in six minutes. All 1,053 Australian prisoners on board were either killed by the torpedoes or drowned in their prison cells below deck.

My uncle, Robert Burrowes, the man after whom I am named, was one of those prisoners. Bob was a soldier in the 34th Fortress Engineers of the Australian Imperial Force. He was captured during the fall of Rabaul on January 22. 1942, held prisoner and half-starved at the Malaguna Road camp until he was put on the Japanese prisoner-of-war ship *Montevideo Maru* in late June.

Assuming he was not killed outright, for six terrifying minutes shortly after midnight on July 1, 1942, my uncle Bob knew he was going to die. I sometimes wonder for how long he was able to hold his breath after his prison cell was submerged: 30 seconds? One minute? Two?

In his final letter home, written while he was a prisoner, Bob wrote "Get Jim out if you possibly can." But it was too late. Bob's brother Jim had already joined up and been assigned to M Special Force; he served as a coastwatcher in Papua New Guinea. After the war he married Beryl, a veteran of the Women's Australian Air Force (WAAF). Jim and Beryl "made" me, as Dad sometimes jokes.

My father's twin brother Tom was a wireless air gunner on a Beaufort bomber—aircraft irreverently, but accurately, known as "flying coffins"—in the RAAF's 100 Squadron. He was shot down over Rabaul on his first mission on December 14, 1943. His plane was never found.

My childhood is dotted with memories of Bob—wearing his war medals to school on ANZAC day, attending memorial services at the Shrine of Remembrance—and Tom. And throughout my childhood I sometimes ask *why* my uncles were killed and *how* war can be ended, but the answers of adults do not satisfy me. And I know that I will have to find out the answers for myself one day.

Sometime in 1962: I am ten years old. I stare in disbelief and fear at the photograph before me. It is on the front page of a newspaper. The photograph is of a starving black child. I am frightened that I live in a world in which adults let children starve. "Why?" I ask my father. "How can this be ended?"

In 1966, the year I turned 14, I decided that I would devote my life to answering two questions: Why are human beings violent? How can this violence be ended? I also decided to act on the basis of what I learned by seeking answers to these two questions. This is more than a life passion: It is why I live.

However, despite more years of school and several at university, which included research designed to answer these two questions, I was still unable to find the answers I was seeking.

January 1983: I stand on the bank of the Gordon River below where it has been joined by the Franklin. I look in bewilderment and horror at the devastated area known as Warner's Landing. I wonder how many birds, mammals, reptiles, insects, trees and plants died in the carnage when the area was clearfelled a few weeks earlier in preparation for the giant dam wall that is to be built here. "Why?" I silently ask myself. "And how can such destruction be ended?" An hour later I am arrested while nonviolently obstructing the work of a bulldozer. I spend four days in jail with several fellow nonviolent activists.

September 9, 1985: I am urgently summoned by a doctor to perform cardio-pulmonary resuscitation (at which I was expertly trained during my years as a lifesaver with The Royal Life Saving Society) on an emaciated three-month old baby girl. The child is a Tigrayan refugee and the location is Shagarab East 3 Refugee Camp in eastern Sudan at the height of the Ethiopian war and famine. I am a volunteer relief worker with a Community Aid Abroad (Oxfam) refugee health team. I carefully monitor my technique on the delicate body of the emaciated child after her distraught mother had been persuaded to surrender the child to let me attempt the resuscitation. I put my heart, soul and years of training into my effort to save the child both for the child's sake and for the sake of her mother. The doctor eventually persuades me that my effort is in vain: the child is dead. I move away to feel my pain and to cry inside. "Why? How?"

January 27, 1991: Earlier today Iraqi officials evacuated the Gulf Peace Team, of which I am a member, from our camp on the border between Iraq and Saudi Arabia. We are now in the Al Rasheed Hotel in central Baghdad. At night I stand in my room looking out of the window. Bombs of the U.S.-led coalition land on the outskirts (and sometimes the suburbs) of Baghdad. The tracer bullets of anti-aircraft fire race into the sky. Five decades after my uncles were killed and now with 25 years of research and ten years of nonviolent activism behind me, I must still ask: "Why? How?"

28

Who am I? I am my two uncles and hundreds of thousands of Iraqis killed in war. I am the wildlife and trees destroyed at Warner's Landing. I am an emaciated African baby girl that has just died despite the effort of this strange-looking white fellow who tried to revive me.

I live in a world of violence. I live in a world of war. I live in a world of poverty among plenty. I live in a world of ecological destruction. And I live in a world of grotesque injustice. Why?

By 1996, with 30 years of research behind me, which included writing *The Strategy of Nonviolent Defense: A Gandhian Approach* http://www.sunypress.edu/p-2176-the-strategy-of-nonviolent-defe.aspx I still could not answer my fundamental question: Why are human beings violent?

At this point, Anita McKone and I decided to go into seclusion so that we could undertake a deep psychological examination of our own minds. Despite my original hope that this would take no more than a couple of years, we did not emerge from seclusion until 2010, 14 years later. Our time in seclusion was frightening, difficult and painful beyond measure. It was also utterly liberating. Because we had minimal financial resources for this extended period, the bulk of which was provided by my very supportive parents James and Beryl Burrowes, we spent the second half of this period in seclusion living in a tent in an isolated forest. Fortunately, the beauty of this location provided us with some relief from the daily horror of uncovering the deeply suppressed and utterly debilitating feelings—fear, sadness, anger, terror, fury, dread, pain—of our childhoods.

Apart from our original motivation, the two things that kept us going during these 14 years in seclusion were our shared commitment to complete the journey and the incredible learning that we experienced. It was, at times, truly breathtaking to gain insight into ourselves that we had never imagined possible: To finally understand *why* we are who we are.

So my journey to understand human violence finally ended in 2010, 44 years after I began it. Here is a brief summary of what Anita and I learned.

Why are Human Beings Violent?

Perpetrators of violence learn their craft in childhood. If you inflict violence on a child, they learn to inflict violence on others. The terrorist suffered violence as a child. The political leader who wages war suffered violence as a child. The man who inflicts violence on women suffered violence as a child. The corporate executive who exploits working class people or those who live in Africa, Asia or Central/South America suffered violence as a child. The individual who perpetrates violence in the home, in the schoolyard or on the street suffered violence as a child.

If we want to end violence, war and exploitation then we must finally end our longest and greatest war: the adult war on children. And here's an incentive: if we do not tackle the fundamental cause of violence, then our combined and unrelenting efforts to tackle all of its other symptoms must ultimately fail. And extinction at our own hand is inevitable.

How can I claim that violence against children is the fundamental cause of all other violence? Consider this. There is universal acceptance that behavior is shaped by childhood experience. If it was not, we would not put such effort into education and other efforts to socialize children to fit into society. And this is why many psychologists have argued that exposure to war toys and violent video games shapes attitudes and behaviors in relation to violence.

But it is far more complex than this and, strange though it may seem, it is not just the "visible" violence (such as hitting, screaming at and sexually abusing) that we normally label "violence" that causes the main damage, although this is extremely damaging. The largest component of damage arises from the "invisible" and "utterly invisible" violence that we adults unconsciously inflict on children during the ordinary course of the day. Tragically, the bulk of this violence occurs in the family home and at school. See "Why Violence?" http://tinyurl.com/whyviolence and "Fearless Psychology and Fearful Psychology: Principles and Practice" http://anitamckone.wordpress.com/articles-2/fearless-and-fearful-psychology/

So what is "invisible" violence? It is the "little things" we do every day, partly because we are just "too busy." For example, when we do not allow time to listen to, and value, a child's thoughts and feelings, the child learns to not listen to him or herself, thus destroying their internal communication system. When we do not let a child say what they want (or ignore them when they do), the child develops communication and behavioral dysfunctionalities as they keep trying to meet their own needs (which, as a basic survival strategy, they are genetically programmed to do).

When we blame, condemn, insult, mock, embarrass, shame, humiliate, taunt, goad, guilt-trip, deceive, lie to, bribe, blackmail, moralize with and/or judge a child, we both undermine their sense of self-worth and teach them to blame, condemn, insult, mock, embarrass, shame, humiliate, taunt, goad, guilt-trip, deceive, lie, bribe, blackmail, moralize and/or judge.

The fundamental outcome of being bombarded throughout their childhood by this "invisible'" violence is that the child is utterly overwhelmed by feelings of fear, pain, anger and sadness (among many others). However, parents, teachers and other adults also actively interfere with the expression of these feelings and the behavioral responses that are naturally generated by them and it is this "utterly invisible" violence that explains why the dysfunctional behavioral outcomes actually occur.

For example, by ignoring a child when they express their feelings, by comforting, reassuring or distracting a child when they express their feelings, by laughing at or ridiculing their feelings, by terrorizing a child into not expressing their feelings (e.g. by screaming at them when they cry or get angry), and/or by violently controlling a behavior that is generated by their feelings (e.g. by hitting them, restraining them or locking them into a room), the child has no choice but to unconsciously suppress their awareness of these feelings.

However, once a child has been terrorized into suppressing their awareness of their feelings (rather than being allowed to have their feelings and to act on them) the child has also unconsciously suppressed their awareness of the reality that caused these feelings. This has many outcomes that are disastrous for the individual, for society and for nature because the individual will now easily suppress their awareness of the feelings that would tell them how to act most functionally in any given circumstance and they will progressively acquire a phenomenal variety of dysfunctional behaviors, including some that are violent towards themselves, others and/or the Earth.

From the above, it should also now be apparent that punishment should never be used. "Punishment," of course, is one of the words we use to obscure our awareness of the fact that we are using violence. Violence, even when we label it "punishment," scares children and adults alike and cannot elicit a functional behavioral response. If someone behaves dysfunctionally, they need to be listened to, deeply, so that they can start to become consciously aware of the feelings (which will always include fear and, often, terror) that drove the dysfunctional behavior in the first place. They then need to feel and express these feelings (including any anger) in a safe way. Only then will behavioral change in the direction of functionality be possible. See "Nisteling: The Art of Deep Listening" http://www.scoop.co.nz/stories/HL1408/S00192/nisteling-the-art-of-deep-listening.htm

"But these adult behaviors you have described don't seem that bad. Can the outcome be as disastrous as you claim?" you might ask. The problem is that there are hundreds of these "ordinary," everyday behaviors that destroy the selfhood of the child. It is "death by a thousand cuts" and most children simply do not survive as self-aware individuals. And why do we do this? We do it so that each child will fit into our model of "the perfect citizen": that is, obedient and hardworking student, reliable and pliant employee/soldier, and submissive law-abiding citizen.

Moreover, once we destroy the selfhood of a child, it has many flow-on effects. For example, once you terrorize a child into accepting certain information about her or himself, other people or the state of the world, the child becomes unconsciously fearful of dealing with new information, especially if this information is contradictory to what they have been terrorized into believing. As a result, the child will unconsciously dismiss new information out of hand. In short, the child has been terrorized in such a way that they are no longer capable of learning (or their learning capacity is seriously diminished by excluding any information that is not a simple extension of what they already "know"). If you imagine any of the bigots you know, you are imagining someone who is utterly terrified. But it's not just the bigots; virtually all people are affected in this manner making them incapable of responding adequately to new information. This is one explanation why some people are "climate deniers."

So if we want to end human violence, we must tackle all of its symptoms simultaneously but, as part of our strategy, we must also tackle the cause. Primarily, this means giving everyone, child and adult alike, all of the space they need to feel, deeply, what they want to do, and to then let them do it (or to have the feelings they naturally have if they are prevented from doing so). In the short term, this will have some dysfunctional outcomes. But it will lead to an infinitely better overall outcome than the system of emotional suppression, control and punishment which has generated the incredibly violent world in which we now find ourselves.

This all sounds pretty unpalatable doesn't it? So each of us has a choice. We can suppress our awareness of what is unpalatable, as we have been terrorized into doing as a child, or we can feel the various feelings that we have in response to this information and then ponder ways forward. If feelings are felt and expressed then our responses can be shaped by the conscious and integrated functioning of thoughts and feelings, as evolution intended, and we can plan intelligently. The alternative is to have our unconscious fear controlling our thinking and deluding us that we are acting rationally.

It is time to end the adult war on children so that all of the other violence that emerges from this cause can end too. So what do we do?

Well, if you are willing, you can make the commitment outlined in "My Promise to Children" http://english.pravda.ru/health/07-11-2013/126076-promise_children-0/. You can also consider participating in "The Flame Tree Project to Save Life on Earth" http://tinyurl.com/flametree which maps out a fifteen-year strategy for creating a peaceful, just and sustainable world community so that all children have an ecologically viable planet on which to live. And, if you like, you can join the worldwide movement to end all violence by signing the online pledge of "The People's Charter to Create a Nonviolent World" http://thepeoplesnonviolencecharter.wordpress.com

Conclusion

In an important sense, what Anita and I learned helped us to understand that ending human violence is impossible. This is because the psychological damage that has been suffered by virtually all of us and, particularly, by serious perpetrators of violence is very difficult to reverse and takes a great deal of time. And the world is not even paying attention to this deep psychological problem nor is it devoting resources to the effort that will be necessary to effectively address it.

Nevertheless, we persevere in the knowledge that what we offer is an important ingredient in the collective effort now being undertaken to avert human extinction and, perhaps, as our multifaceted crises deepen, more people will be inclined to look more deeply.

Anyway, while a world without violence might not be possible, we humans are always undertaking things that look impossible at first glance. The point, as my parents taught me, is to "Try. Try again." I still do. And, at 92, they are still my greatest supporters.

Understanding human violence is one thing, ending it another. Will you help us?

Robert J. Burrowes has a lifetime commitment to understanding and ending human violence. He has done extensive research since 1966 in an effort to understand why human beings are violent and has been a nonviolent activist since 1981. He is the author of "Why Violence?" http://tinyurl.com/whyviolence His email address is flametree@riseup.net and his website is at http://robertjburrowes.wordpress.com

Marianna Perez de Fransius

Making Peace Sexy

While in my third year of university in late 2000, I applied for the Circumnavigators Fellowship, an $8,000 grant to spend the summer traveling around the world. The only parameters were that the itinerary had to include at least three continents and six countries. So I wrote a proposal to research peacebuilding and reconciliation projects that used cultural expression. I found a theater company in Northern Ireland that worked with Catholics and Protestants, a dance troupe in Kashmir that brought together Indians and Pakistanis and an Indonesian shadow puppetry group that addressed difficult issues with minority groups. I didn't get the grant (the selection committee thought I had too many potentially dangerous locations), but I did gain a passion for peacebuilding and conflict transformation. In doing the application process, I realized that I knew quite a bit about international relations and other countries, but very little about peace. This struck me as a little bizarre considering the fact that I was studying in a prestigious international affairs program which prides itself on having educated many past, present and future world leaders. And after all, shouldn't world leaders be utmostly concerned with peace?

So I decided to go and get a Master's Degree in Peace Studies at a little known university in the Austrian countryside. We were 40 students from 25 countries all living in the same house. When we weren't in class, we were trying to implement what we'd learned—it was very experiential, to say the least. When I tell people that I have a degree in Peace Studies, the reaction is invariably one of surprise and/or gratitude. "I didn't even know you could study peace!" "I could never do that! But I'm glad that someone is doing it. It's so needed." Ironically, my biggest challenge hasn't been around any of the conflict transformation work that I've done since gaining my degree, but something much more fundamental: convincing people that peace is possible, powerful and accessible.

While people the world over are surprised and grateful—I like to flatter myself in thinking—that I've chosen to study and work in the field of peace, in the United States, I've encountered a very particular mix of reactions which I think has a lot to do with how peace got branded in the 1960s. Firstly, most of the people that I met working—or more accurately volunteering—for peace were women and some men who had earned their stripes in the protests of the 1960s as hippies. So already, there was a predisposition to go out and be *against* something, namely war. Many were angry, frustrated and in despair that despite all their efforts wars hadn't been eradicated, and now there was terrorism to contend with too.

Mixed in with these doubts there was a question about whether peace really is a powerful stance. I'm not sure when this bit of how history is taught entered the curriculum in the US, but people would often tell me, "What about the time that the world made peace by giving Hitler the Sudentenland? He then just took more and more and more and killed six million people along the way. Clearly peace just ends up in war." Interestingly, I never get this argument in Europe, where people were much more directly affected by Hitler's actions. I actually wonder if it's a narrative that emerged during the Cold War as a way of justifying the U.S. government's nuclear weapons program.

But perhaps the greatest challenge is convincing "normal," everyday people that peace is accessible to them. Whether it's on the inner peace or interpersonal peace or international peace levels, most people don't realize that they can, and in fact are, participating in creating peace. Peace seems to be relegated to Buddhist monks or diplomats.

With that in mind, I started Peace is Sexy (www.peaceissexy.net) which offers original content with the objective of re-branding peace as sexy, possible, profitable and fun. Essentially, I am telling stories of "normal" people accessing peace in their particular way, whether it is teaching yoga, organizing soccer tournaments or lobbying for the UN Resolution to ban small weapons. And perhaps out of the desire to show the intersection of inner, interpersonal and international levels of peace I wrote "The Dreaded Conversation Workbook: Participate in Dreaded Conversations with Ease." It started as a means of helping people achieve some inner and interpersonal peace in recurring conversations about big, controversial international issues, but I have since seen it applied in many other contexts, whether it's in the workplace, at home or in community organizations.

All this to say that not only can you study peace, but you can also implement it in your daily life. While the fields of peace studies, conflict transformation, community relations, corporate social responsibility, social justice, human rights etc. have all made huge strides since I applied for that Circumnavigators' Fellowship, it seems that we're still holding on to a cultural conception of peace from the 1960s. I was recently invited to speak at Build Peace, a conference on technology and peacebuilding about creating digital games for peace—difficult to get more modern or forward looking. A few weeks ahead of the conference, the organizers (all in their 20s and 30s) sent out a blogpost that included a suggested soundtrack for the event. The blogpost was aptly titled "The

Song Remains the Same" and half the songs on the playlist were from the 1960s (Bob Dylan, the Doors, Phil Ochs…). The more recent songs were from obscure artists and certainly weren't culturally significant. It makes me think that the big re-branding of peace that I'm trying to catalyze won't happen until some widely culturally significant artists start creating some new anthems that show peace as sexy, possible, profitable and fun.

Marianne Perez de Fransius helps people see the value of peace in their daily lives so that we can all live in a better world. She does this by rebranding peace as sexy, possible, profitable, and fun; teaching middle school kids peace and conflict transformation skills through video games, and helping parents travel the world with their babies. Marianne never felt that she fit in because she was born in Brazil of a French father and an American mother and was brought up in the Sephardic Jewish tradition. But growing up in a multicultural household and experiencing an international education, Marianne has seen over and over again the power of people to connect despite all their differences. Her bachelor's degree is in international relations from Georgetown University's School of Foreign Service and her master's is in peace and conflict studies from the European Peace University where her thesis was on "Moving Mainstream Media Towards a Culture of Peace." Marianne is also the author of "The Dreaded Conversation Workbook: Navigate Dreaded Conversations with Ease."

Christina Kieltyka

Passion for the Beloved Earth

In the early '70s, in an earth science class at Iowa State University, I found out that others were concerned about the health of the earth. They essentially said that our planet was on the cusp of crisis. Ecologically we were out of balance and heading for worse. I had already intuited this; my soul had known it for some time, but it somehow helped to know that there were people out there not only demonstrating for peace but working to enlighten our culture about the earth. Scientists like Wes Jackson in Kansas, who founded The Land Institute, was working on perennial crops to feed our gargantuan appetites and Francis Lappe, author of *Diet for a Small Planet,* who spoke for the U.N. Health organization at a huge symposium, explaining that there was enough food for all, that it was about what we ate and who had access to food for a healthful diet. Barbara Kingsolver put in her talent, Edward Abby, Alice Walker, Aldo Leopold, Gary Snyder, Joni Mitchell—so many great talents were taking up the fight. It was heady and it was right. There is a higher power than governments, a higher law, and social and ecological justice spoke to the journey I was already on.

In 1980 I was finally free to join wholeheartedly in the back-to-the-land movement, *five acres and independence,* living simply, lovingly with the earth and each other in community. For nearly 20 years I lived and worked and bartered. Stained glass or other artwork paid dentist and doctor bills for me and my family. We home schooled, and shared this undertaking with other families with similar life views. We traded our work for any food I couldn't grow. We worked toward a 10-year moratorium against mining in Wisconsin; we worked for fair wages for all and for food that reflected the real price of fresh picked ripe, organic food. It was good and whole and right. In 1998 my husband no longer wanted to be married and to keep the old house we had so lovingly restored to beauty. This was a major life-changing event: moving back to Iowa State to finish a graduate degree, teaching a full load of three classes, living and renting in town, and becoming a single mom.

How did I combine my passion for the beloved earth with my belief that for every act of social injustice there were acts of ecological injustice that laid the groundwork for all future abuse? (One only has to look at the coal and oil industries, the burgeoning power of Monsanto, the abuses of migrant workers in Florida and elsewhere. Desecration of the earth for profit is killing us.) As a longtime Quaker, I was comfortable with silence and self-questioning, with group discernment and testimonies of peace, simplicity and integrity, and with the belief that there is that of the sacred in each person and in all beings sharing this planet, so I started there. I was so fortunate that educators like Peter Elbow and his famous "free-writing" and Parker Palmer were writing and lecturing. While there was the insanity of Bush-ites in education, there was also another revolution brewing in teachers' hearts. I taught writing, all kinds of writing and literature, and while I seldom mentioned politics, I deliberately chose short stories by Alice Walker, James Baldwin, Louise Erdrich, essays by Rachel Carson, Barry Lopez, Sigurd Olson, Wendell Berry, Susan Griffin, poetry by

W.S Merwin, Adrienne Rich, William Heyen. These essays were genuinely well written by well-respected authors and they were in the textbooks, so if I pulled them out to use as models of good description, good use of concrete examples, of balance with ethos, pathos, logos, of argument or persuasion, of whatever a particular course called for, who could fault me? I am a good teacher and I was doing my job.

If, on the other hand, there was a sub-text going on, I admit it. Peter Elbow gave me—and all educators—the right to pull silence into our classrooms. We would start simply. I would tell my students that these exercises were graded according to ability to think critically, to be able to support an argument or idea with facts, good examples, with thorough reasoning. I did not take off for punctuation or spelling or even lack of organization. Just write, I'd tell them, without phones or music, starting at five minutes, eventually working up to 20 or more when developing more organized drafts. An example. We read "Sr. Flowers" by Maya Angelou. We analyzed her excellent use of description, i.e., lips the color of ripe plums, her house with gently blowing soft white curtains and the scent of cinnamon from the thin, crisp, lightly browned cookies sitting on the table. We talked about how and why Sr. Flowers was so important to this young child. Then we followed with the prompt (known in Quaker circles as a query: Have you had mentors in your life? Who? Write only what you are comfortable with having me and others read and no examples of drug use or explicit sex (I'd usually get a laugh with that). But what, I'd ask, did this person teach you and why does it matter now? Will you hand this on? Write down the prompts and go with any or all or bits and pieces. It's your creative and critical thinking I am interested in.

Silence, writing, some groaning and moaning at first, a little outright rebellion which I told them to write about respectfully. Eventually this became an expected part of class and if other teachers weren't doing things this way, well, I was heartily supported by any and all contemporary magazines and programs from on high. We did some incredible writing and it was an uphill battle because I had ended up teaching in a bible-belt, shelled-out mining community, rife with orange, dead, clogged streams from mine run-off, lack of education or respect for education, almost a fear of it, along with high unemployment and unsafe, low paying jobs, no health insurance, the highest incidence of familial abuse, and drug and alcohol abuse in the state of Iowa.

I was accused of being a witch (a fireable offense there—it would just be called something else) and of being a femi-Nazi. I was backed against the wall of the Post Office and yelled at for putting up an Obama sign in my yard. Often I heard gun shots at night and my dog learned quickly who was on meth when they banged on my door at night. While I was respected professionally, my work to educate city councils was met with anger, the mayor calling me a "goddam hippy chick and outsider" to boot. He also accused me of using "professor language" and that I wasn't a bit better than him, etc. Of course, I do want to admit, and with a smile, that after a year or two of dealing with me, and a little smokin' out in my driveway, he actually asked me to be his running mate for city council, said I was probably the best one they ever had, kind of hinted that he was sorry he had put up so much resistance at first. He added, "Who'd a thunk it? An old hippy chick and an old biker…and we're a darn good team." But by then I was ill and moving on.

So my journey took some radical, sometimes difficult, turns and changes. I had two wonderful years of teaching at a small private college where my colleagues were talented educators and writers, where they considered it part of the job to write, and we were given support in doing this. But I was having health issues and I'd had to commute too far, so I had ended up coming back to the little junior college where I had been before, where academic excellence was a phrase they might have heard somewhere but did not practice (pass the ball players, no matter what, or pass your colleague's lazy son if you want don't want to be ostracized, and so on). Still, I had started a pre-school reading program that, last I heard, is still going. I had wonderful students that I still value. I had the most beautiful yards and gardens, had restored one acre of prairie, had met wonderful, laugh-filled gorgeous people that had few teeth, went barefoot (most often from choice), who gathered herbs and berries, put up preserves according to season, who invited me to their homes where there might be holes in the floor and a stock tank for bathing in the bathroom, who shoveled my walks in the winter, and who brought roses to plant or lilacs for the table, and who sat on my patio, drank wine, watched the stars come out, and who told stories. I came to the conclusion over the years that wealth and beauty are inside of us, and that our testimonies are not what we say we believe in. They are what we live, the choices we make. They are what we *do*.

Christina Kieltyka I raised three sons in western Wisconsin, but now live in South Minneapolis with my oldest son and his wife. My social and eco justice activism and my spiritual life have always been directly tied to my love of the earth and always to a deep sense of place. Because of health issues, I no longer hike or live largely out of doors. Because of this, the content and colors of my paintings changed radically. There are still connections to the earth, community, and living simply with integrity, daily blessing and gratitude.

My activism changed to doing such gentle things as after-school mentoring, mostly through writing and art, and eventually, to only my writing and art where I wish to express a sense of urgency about the choices we are making alongside the necessity of listening to the wisdom of original instruction from traditional teachers.

I have exhibited at Powderhorn Art Fair, the Cedar Cultural Arts Center, Women's Art Festival, the Craftastic women, at The Loft's Peace and Social Justice Writing Group's presentation in 2013, the TCFM art fair, and other places as well. In 2003 I was nominated for the Pushcart Prize for Poetry, and have been the recipient of arts grants in three states. I am a Quaker and a pagan, a poet and a visual artist, a mom and teacher/gardener/student. My paintings are my journey, my story, my acts of faith and prayer.
www.christinakart.com

Svetlana Kim

How I Survived in America with One Dollar and One Dream

I hope that all of you realize and exploit the larger opportunity here on the Earth.

I am excited for this opportunity to share my lessons about overcoming obstacles, and my belief in pursuing impossible dreams, and letting creativity and intuition help you to realize your dreams. Do you want to finish your manuscript? Do you need an idea to create a pitch or proposal? How to get a good idea?

My grandmother always reminds me, "Anything is possible." I arrived in New York City on December 18, 1991, with literally one dollar in my pocket. I had one dollar, and a dream. I didn't speak a single word of English. I didn't have a rich aunt or uncle to greet me at the airport. I had no place to stay. I tell you this because I know very well what it means not to have a steady job, and to have to clean restrooms for five dollars a day. I know what it's like to have no change for bus fare, and to go hungry for three days. I know what it means when fear controls your life.

Fear. It is one of the greatest obstacles to achieving success. There's no number—no limit—to the kinds of fears we must face every day. And just think about the damage unchecked fear does to us. Think about the tremendous energy we waste just thinking about fear! Does it really deserve that much attention? No! That's why I call fear a "spoiled child"—it takes and takes, distracting us from our real goals.

When I came to America, I did so with an open-date airline ticket. After three difficult months in American, the night before my return ticket to Russia was due to expire, I didn't sleep at all. My pillow was wet with tears. This was my last chance to go home. Making decisions is difficult, but making a decision that will affect your life once and forever is nearly impossible. I agonized all night long.

My flight was leaving at nine o'clock the next morning. When morning came, I made a cup of coffee and went outside. But instead of heading for the airport, I took the first bus I saw and ended up in a nice part of the city, where I saw a woman pushing a stroller. On impulse, I followed her. A block later, she entered a building and posted a note on an announcement board: Nanny wanted.

I could read her note! Even though I still knew very little English, I understood what this woman was advertising for. "Nanny" in English sounds like the Russian word, "Nannya." I understood that she needed some help. But when I turned around, she was gone. I ran outside, screaming, "Hello! Hello!" The woman stopped. I did my very best to speak good English—and I got the nanny job!

I came to America, like so many others, because I believed in the words of the Declaration of Independence: That "all men are created equal" and that they have incredible rights—including "life, liberty, and the pursuit of happiness." I had faith in the American dream: a faith in things unseen, the courage to embrace one's fear. I had many fears, but my dream was bigger than my fear. I learned to embrace my fear, and to release it.

My greatest inspiration through every difficulty I've faced is my paternal grandmother, *Bya-ok*, which is Korean for "White Pearl." She has always believed that I can do, be, and have anything I want if I dream big, and pursue those dreams.

The word "failure" did not exist in White Pearl's vocabulary. Instead, she called life's difficulties and challenges "life lessons." I once read that every single pearl evolves from a central core. This core is simply an irritant—a fragment of shell or fishbone, a grain of sand. To protect itself from this irritant, the oyster secretes multiple layers of nacre, which, over time, form a beautiful pearl. I think of this process when I think of my grandmother: She experienced some very difficult events in her own life, but despite it all, she became one of the rarest and most beautiful of pearls.

My grandmother's parents were the first generation of what we call *Koryo-Saram*, which means "Korean person," the people who came to Russia during the Joseon dynasty. They came to Russia in 1900, after a poor harvest and famine in Korea, to pursue a better life. They were country people, very down-to-earth and hard-working. They had no electricity or plumbing, no bath or shower. These are the people White Pearl and I are descended from—people of courage, of tenacity.

The wisdom of White Pearl's parents was passed down to my grandmother, who passed it down to me. Now I want to pass this wisdom to you. I want to share seven life lessons I've learned from White Pearl, and have mastered on my own. I still apply her lessons to every situation I face today. Her wisdom kept me strong and kept me going. I am who I am today because of the lessons I learned and lived.

As White Pearl would say, "Face every situation with faith, hope, and love. Embrace all that life throws at you, good or bad; neither will last forever. Life is a gift from God, and it's up to you how to use it." Now I will share with you the secrets of White Pearl's wisdom:

Step 1: Embrace serendipity.

My life is often a string of serendipitous events and good fortune. And sometimes, when you embrace serendipity, you achieve greater dreams than you dared to expect or hope for.

Just as serendipity helped me get my first job as a nanny in America, it also set off a chain of events that helped me write my first book. When I first moved to Washington, D.C., in January of 2006, I met a woman named Jean C. Palmer. Jean was surprised to hear my Russian accent—she wasn't the first one, and won't be the last! I told her the story of my ancestors: How they moved from Korea to Russia 106 years ago to escape famine; how, in 1937, Stalin designated all ethnic Koreans enemies of the State and with barely a day's notice, had people packed into cattle trains and forcefully deported.

I also told Jean about my own journey to America—how I was a fourth generation of Koreans raised in Russia, and how I dreamed of coming to America, and made that dream come true. I told her about the single dollar in my pocket when I arrived in this country, and about the difficulties I faced and trials I went through—and how all of this resulted in me being hired as a stockbroker and, eventually, moving to Washington. Jean looked at me with astonishment and said, "You must write a book! You must write your book."

Serendipitously, after Jean's encouragement, I met a surprising number of great writers. They walked into my life at seemingly random moments, and each one asked me, "Are you writing a book?"

Jean connected me with her friend, Sam Horn, bestselling author of *POP! Stand Out in a Crowd*. Sam also believed I had a story to tell, and she invited me to her house in Virginia. But two weeks after my first conversation with her, I received a blow: The company I worked for had closed my department; I was without a job.

I sat at my desk, closed my eyes, and took a deep breath. I was saddened, but my guts told me that this was the best thing that could happen to me. I cleaned my office and organized all my files, making sure that there were no bills left for my clients. Then I walked into the CEO's office, calm and with a smile on my face. I told them that I was grateful for the promotion I had received two weeks before, but that I had recently been considering my resignation because I wanted to complete the manuscript that I had begun to write.

They were surprised but appreciative of my work for them. The offered me a severance package, and even joked that I should have my own TV show.

I began to write my book. Life had brought me serendipity, disguised as difficulty!

Serendipity had brought Sam Horn into my life, and she encouraged me. I told her about the time I purchased cat food at a Safeway for my dinner. We eat a lot of canned food in Russia. In Russia, we didn't have bread—and here, in America, I discover food for cats, in a can! Sam said, "This story goes in your book." I told her about the time I deposited my first check into a trash slot at Wells Fargo bank because I'd never send or used an ATM before. "It goes in the book," Sam said. "Oh, no," I said. "I will look silly." I was laughing—but I put it in the book!

Serendipity also led me to two more important friends: John Tullius and Ron Powers. One day, while looking at Sam's website, I read a post about the Maui Writers Conference. Sam encouraged me to submit my manuscript—but the deadline was that very day! I submitted fifteen rough pages and a synopsis about my potential book. In less than an hour, John Tullius, the founder of the conference wrote to me: "I love the story of the breadline and the mafia guy in the fancy car scalping airline tickets! But each scene needs to be more fully exploited." He gave me advice about including details, and conveying the challenges I faced as a young girl struggling to find my dream. He advised me on how to expand twenty pages of manuscript to fifty, seventy, even one hundred.

Finally, he said, "Pour your heart out to me. I am your reader. I want to crawl inside your heart. Let me know every intimate detail, even the stuff you don't want to tell. Then you'll have written a blockbuster sensation that people will want to talk about. Remember one thing you write: Fear nothing."

In Hawaii, at the conference, though, I was not myself. Suddenly, my confidence was gone, and my attitude diminished. All my classmates were seasoned writers and had completed manuscripts. And twenty minutes before class, I discovered the worst: My name wasn't on the list!

The instructor, Ron Powers—the Pulitzer Prize-winning author of *Flags of Our Fathers* and *Mark Twain: A Life*—allowed me to sit beside him in class, despite the fact that I was not on the list. The next day, he arranged for me to officially be in the class. After my graduation, we became friends.

He told me, "The best way to write is to write, write, write and to read, read, read." He urged me to interview White Pearl. When the conference and workshop were over, I flew to Washington, D.C., went home, switched my luggage, and was on my way to the airport to visit and interview White Pearl. Writing my book, I learned more about my grandmother and my family than I ever thought I would. When I finished my book, my grandmother said to me, "Thank you for your courage for giving voice to my people." My vision for a book was bigger than receiving royalties. I wanted to share the story of 480,000 ethnic Koreans who live in the former Soviet Union today. Until the era of glasnost and perestroika, the topic of the forceful deportation of Soviet Koreans was prohibited.

Serendipity led me to the people who inspired me to include my own story of success—and the story of my grandmother, and of the Soviet Koreans. And with my grandmother's permission, the photographs that I used in my book were donated to the Asian Division of the Library of Congress. Soon, there will be a new collection, and all the future studies and books on the topic of ethnic Koreans in Russia will be added to that collection.

Step 2: *Recognize and face opportunities with faith, hope and love.*

I believe that opportunities exist everywhere. Even today's global recession represents unprecedented opportunity for growth and innovation. Behind a crisis is the greatest opportunity, and endless possibility. Taking the opportunity is hard-wired into many of you, and often emerges at an early age. One of my all-time favorite quotes by John F. Kennedy is, "The Chinese use two brush strokes to write the word 'crisis.' One brush stroke is for 'danger;' the other is for 'opportunity.' In a crisis, be aware of the danger, but recognize the opportunity."

My father taught me to see and seize opportunities, even the small ones. And sometimes perhaps a small one will lead to a larger one.

It was December of 1991 in Leningrad, Russia. It all started with a loaf of bread that didn't even exist. I stood waiting in a bread line at the local bakery for the third day in a row. It was just three short months before the collapse of the Soviet Union. Little did I know how much my own life was about to change.

A black Mercedes had pulled up to the curb. The driver rolled down the window and yelled, "People! Do we have bread or do we have to eat potatoes?"

Who did I see at the wheel of this fancy car but my old classmate, Vladimir! Even though it was a gray winter day, he was wearing oversized, too-cool-for-school Versace sunglasses. The expensive car, the expensive glasses—all at once, I knew: He was Russian mafia!

Vladimir was selling airline tickets to America on the black market. He said he had one ticket to New York City. Regardless of the price, my first impulse was to say, "I'll take it!" But immediately, my mind flooded with concerns and fears. Where could I get the money? How could I abandon my family and friends, and the only life I knew?

But I was suddenly determined to pull it off. "I want the ticket," I told Vladimir, projecting a bravado I did not fully feel. "It's a done deal," I told him, not even knowing where I would find the money. But I knew that I would find it—this was the opportunity of a lifetime! How did I know? I listened to my intuition—it's the closest thing to my creator. Even today I follow the same principle.

To my surprise, Vladimir said in an unfriendly voice, "The deal is not done until I have the cash in my hands."

I raced off on my mission to somehow collect the money, pack my clothes, and pray for a visa. I borrowed money from my parents and my friends. I was waiting for Vladimir three hours before the flight, with cash in my hands...and he wasn't there. He was running late! Finally, he showed up, and I handed him a pile of cash. He counted it.

"You are one thousand rubles short," he said.

"Oh, no!" I cried. "Vladimir! No one else will buy your ticket—the flight leaves in three hours! How can you do this to me?"

He was cold. "I need the rest of the money if you want this ticket."

I was in tears. Finally, I promised that my mother would give him the rest. He had all the money I had borrowed, and he rolled up the window and drove away. After all of that, I had one dollar left to my name. Just one dollar and a dream.

I believe that opportunities exist all the time, no matter where you live. In fact, I hope you see the opportunity right here at this moment.

You and I—we are people who believe that dreams do come true. We work hard, and that hard work pays off. Trust that anything that happens, happens for a reason. The reason is to learn a lesson. You and I are meant to be together today. There is a reason.

Step 3: Cultivate ultimate optimism.

Let me ask you a question: Do you want to help someone who is complaining about what has happened to him, or someone who is optimistic about his future? I think that optimism is a decision: Once you've made your decision to look up, optimism creates an irresistible magnetism inside of you. By deciding to be optimistic, you can build a successful business, a new life, you can have loving relationships—how you think and act today will create your outcome for tomorrow.

My friend, Sarah Miller Caldicott, great-grandniece of Thomas Edison, wrote a book called *Innovate Like Edison.* Edison cultivated a "charismatic optimism." As he "became a national figure, his positive outlook had an even broader effect. He helped to encourage the nation through tough times. People from all walks of life were uplifted when he said, 'Be courageous. I have seen many depressions in business. Always, America has emerged from these stronger and more prosperous. Be as brave as your fathers before you. Have faith! Go forward!'"

I learned from my grandparents to remain optimistic even when a situation appears catastrophic. I was at the Pulkovo International Airport in Leningrad. I stood in line to get on a shuttle which would take me to the airplane to America. I could not believe all that had happened to me in the last few days— from collecting all that cash for Vladimir, to rushing to obtain a visa, to convincing my mom to send more money to Vladimir— to being robbed on my way to the American Consulate in Moscow! A gift from my grandmother, gold earrings and a necklace, had been stolen from me. Was this all just bad luck?

Looking up as I stood in line, I saw thousands of stars like white pearls all over the sky. It was maybe the darkest night of my life. But Charles A. Beard, one of the most influential American historians of the 20th century once wrote, "When it's dark enough, you can see stars." And my grandfather would often say to me that a starry night meant a great day tomorrow. My fond memories of my grandfather began to calm me down.

As a child, I loved sitting on the porch with him to stargaze. I had always admired his optimism, and I missed being with him most of all. He didn't make a particular effort to be optimistic—he was graced with optimism. He looked on the bright side of everything.

My grandparents, like many other Korean families, were exiled to Chechnya in 1953. Halfway there, my grandfather was struck by a train. My father remembered the enormity of the train, how the wheels were taller than he was at age seven. The bolts were as big as his fist. The wheel cut off my grandfather's left arm. He was unconscious for weeks, and the family prepared for his funeral. But he survived! "I am not disabled," my grandfather told the doctor in the hospital when he regained consciousness. "This is just a little inconvenience."

He refused a disability pension, and when he finally arrived in Chechnya, he built a collective farm, and then was offered a position as a senior agriculturist and awarded with the Order of the Badge of Honor for his work. White Pearl remembers that he never complained, continuing to work long hours. As one of the best senior agriculturists, he was selected to go to Moscow every year to visit an exhibit of national economic achievements. His team became one of the top producing teams in his region.

Like my grandfather, optimists are can-do-it people. They focus on solutions, not problems. Optimists think about what could be done differently next time, what lesson did I learn here—rather than what and why it happened to me, and who is to blame. When we begin to identify every lesson we learn in every difficulty we face, we begin to move ahead faster than ever before.

We all have to make decisions. Optimism can be mastered. Optimism is a choice. Start today with an experiment: Expect something good to happen to you. Right now. Right here. Change does not happen overnight; it happens in small increments, when we decide to make a change. One day, one hour, one minute, one moment at a time. It is in your hands.

Svetlana Kim is a speaker, author, columnist for PERREAULT Global Consciousness magazine, consultant, community advocate, and a host of the radio show "To the Stars through Adversity." She also co-authored *The Last of the Four Musketeers: Allen Joe's Life and Friendship with Bruce Lee,*

Her book *White Pearl and I: A Memoir of a Political Refugee* chronicles her journey from Russia to the United States, where she arrived with only one dollar in her pocket and not a single word of English. Today, she is a leader in the business world, and has been honored with numerous awards citing her commitment, skill, and integrity. Through it all, when her nerve threatens to fail her, she returns to memories of her grandmother, White Pearl, whose parents immigrated to Russia from Korea. As a girl, White Pearl was among 200,000 Soviet Koreans deported to central Asia by Joseph Stalin, who feared they would spy on behalf of the Japanese.

Svetlana Kim was selected to be a spokesperson for the 2011 Macy's Asian Pacific American Heritage Month. Svetlana Kim is also a recipient of the NAAAP 100 Award and was honored in 2010 with the Orphan International Worldwide Global Citizenship Award for her contribution to saving the lives of children in Haiti.

She received the Artemis Award from the Euro-American Women's Council in Athens at the Zappeion Megaron under the auspices of the Ministry of Foreign Affairs and Ministry of Culture of Greece in 2009. She is a recipient of the "Hellenic Award" from The Hon. Nikitas Kaklamanis, Mayor of Athens, Greece.

. In 2008, Kim became an Asian Academy Hall of Fame inductee. In 2009, Svetlana was recognized with the Daily Point of Light Award by the Points of Light Institute created by the administration of President George H.B. Bush to honor individuals creating meaningful change in communities across America. Kim has been featured in *The New York Times, The Wall Street Journal, The Washington Post, The Huffington Post, MSN Money, MSNBC, Women's Life* magazine in Seoul, Korea; the *Asian Fortune*; *Networking Times*; NASDAQ's Closing Bell; and *The Gazette*, a publication of the Library of Congress.

Amanda Lewis

Turning Points and Mrs. Dundee

Dedicated to Mrs. Dundee

Windows : from the outside looking in—the depressive view. Trapped in a never-ending circle—will I ever again break out into joy? I've always assumed that coming to a turning point was a positive refocusing of strength and energy in life, until I found myself running round and round on the inside of that never-ending circle. I began to see that every morning is another marathon of searching for that hidden opening, that wonderful ticket into my freedom and creativity. Certain individuals accuse me of being negative. I always respond that just because someone can see the negative doesn't mean they are the negative.

I never dreamed my life would be like this and that I would be sitting here now. In fact, one needs to acknowledge its presence in order to do anything about it. My body is wracked with pain. I am crippled from my forced labor, and am poorer than hell. I've been a refugee in my own country along with my precious young daughter for years now. I hope I regain the use of my right arm and hand through the healing action of telling my story.

At first, I honestly believed that people would care. I honestly *believed* that, with all of the millions of people out there, that nobody, especially me and my daughter, would ever be allowed to fall through the cracks. My faith was high. *Very* high. Although I felt petrified at the very real possibility of being out on the street, I figured that someone, *somewhere*, would stop something so horrible from happening to me and my child. We are such very good people. We have devoted so much time and effort helping others, and in so many ways. We just *knew* we would be saved—that someone would intervene, and help walk us through this miserable situation.

After all, it wasn't our fault. Someone sorely let us down, abandoned the entire family. Someone we loved and trusted. Someone with whom we had put much time and energy and service and commitment. Someone close to us who, for many reasons, became very, very weak, fearful and dangerous.

With Mrs. Dundee, though, there is still some kind of connection, some kind of true affection flowing among the three of us, even though there was a business aspect of our friendship. We are still behind on rent, often hungry for days at a time, facing the loss of phones, heat, lights, hot water, etc. I recall the evening my vehicle broke down. Mrs. Dundee drove down to the service station. I was inside peeking at the animals to make sure they were doing all right. I turned around to see she had an envelope full of $100 bills to be used to repair my vehicle. I knew I would be able to pay her back with labor. Mrs. Dundee did not want the money back, but her husband back home did. He said to her, "You're never gonna see that money again." She cried as she handed the envelope to me, saying, "I could never do what you are doing." She told me I looked great, like I was just going out to buy a loaf of bread. Does this change my viewpoint about rich people? Not really. For she married into her wealth and was very apologetic for it. Her prayer for us was "thinking good thoughts," which probably does more good than most people's "prayers." The three of us and her little boy had lots of fun together, which broke up the monotony and the fear. The Dundees moved back home overseas and we lost touch. All my energy was now reserved for surviving. The campground was deserted and we were alone down there with crickets and birds and frogs. The next day was fabulous weather. I turned to my daughter and asked, "Do you know how lucky you are to be going through this and to be down here today? There is not a more beautiful place on earth and I wish we could stay here forever."

My body holds out only for as much as we are doing, which is fine because we can only find a few people to work for. The rest are disgusting to me. I type this slowly. I have mostly lost the use of my right arm, hand and shoulder. Ouch!! Thank God I can still *type*.

It has been interesting to watch the rich people respond to the terrorism scare. They are scrambling about, trying to make their materialistic situations still work for them, so dependent on everything external. I've always said that eventually, when we would all have to get our spiritual houses in order, that the rich would be headed for the nearest bridge—that they were so *weak* they would never survive. After how rotten they have treated me and my child, not to mention everyone else they come into contact with, it is a comedy act to *watch* them. They don't know *what* the hell to do.

They don't have a clue what it's like to be exhausted from a long work day, then run errands, then get a surge of happiness to be going home to rest—but whoa! I forgot! We don't have that anymore. We're sleeping right where we're sitting—in our old compact car.

Nobody ever taught me how to live. I had to find that out by myself. By far the most compelling turning point was my decision to face my family of origin's illness of addiction, after seeing for some time that it was threaded through every aspect of my life. Yet the turning point is not easy for it is a constant flow of healing options to choose from, the pain having covered the joy for so long now. Note: emotional highs are not necessarily the same as joy.

Oh, don't get me wrong. I'm no saint. But I do have my morals. Copping out on my child is something I would just never do. But, then *I'm* not *weak*. Evidently I pick weak men or, worse than that, they get weak after knowing me.

Now we have been semi-settled for going on one year. My body is still wracked with pain 24 hours a day. We are still laboring for the exploitative wealthy, but only for people in special situations, not the idle, shallow-minded rich.

It was a cool evening in the late summer. We stopped by the gatehouse to pay our camping fee for the night. We stood side by side, silently watching as a foggy mist-filled canopy formed over the cool night air, mingling with the remaining warmth of the day.

Down with the other campers, a shrill squawk brought us to attention. Four or five tents down, there he was—a stunning bright white parrot, a cockatoo happily preening while getting ready for bed. A sleek white Labrador appeared, obviously happy and content to be hanging out with his people. I wondered where they finally landed after losing their home a couple months back. Obviously they had not intended this sad outcome.

In my mind there are two kinds of addicts. The one in recovery and the one *not* in recovery. The same goes for co-dependency. Recovery has helped me give up the numbing activities and behaviors—and uncover the joy within. Without it, I wouldn't have been strong enough to leave my destructive relationships behind. Believe it or not, this is better. Life is real, focused on living in the moment somehow or not, like when we're all in the car together, joyfully singing and free of fear.

It's like feeling what it's like to clean a deep emotional wound. You try and you try and you try but you just don't seem to rid yourself of the stubborn scab. We get the message from those who have gone before. Polished wisdom, waiting to be shared. No wonder we keep ourselves so separate, so distant from one another, accused of being negative just because we see the negative—the blatant darkness that our society has allowed. We keep doing the same things over and over and over and expecting a different outcome. Addictions hide the conscience and the pain it brings with it.

This is the part that leaves some men weak. Male or female, recovery can leave you temporarily feeling weak. It's not a macho affair. It is actually quite gentle. This, along with an intense personality, can add a stiff dose of humility. My male companions have gone into recovery macho and stayed in recovery humble.

Some have questioned why I keep the animals with us. I say to them that animals are the mirrors of our soul. Animals. They are us. They represent us in the heavens. Their suffering is our suffering. With God's animals, perfection is always shining back at us, telling us what to do. Having come to us as "hard to place" rescues several years ago, how could I abandon them now? More than once my child asked if we gave up the animals when things got harder, would I leave her behind next? My child trusts me because of my actions. Her birth father hasn't been able to give her that gift. And now, we ALL need rescuing.

I discovered something very important in writing this. I discovered once again how deeply I live my life and always have. It seems I always long to go deeper, searching for more meaning, more clarity. I want my work to be read and acknowledged, not because of my ego, but to help people get together for the sake of breaking the isolation. If I can draw myself out of isolation and help heal other broken people, myself included, we could heal all of our differences and meaningless escapades, which greatly drain our energy. In living my life and traveling about, I see that each person or group of people has one thing in common: isolation. Sometimes isolation is better than the companionship available. I'm much more comfortable with fiction and with my novel because there is enough space to allow clarification and get a more accurate picture of my story.

In closing, I believe my main thoughts and feelings revolve around gratitude. My animal-loving friends helped out at times by keeping them in their home if the weather was too hot or too cold or was too wet, and threw in showers for us to boot! When your friend meets you at her door, plugging her nose with her fingers, you know you've got a problem. We all laughed.

Oh, it's just another tidbit from the school of the homeless. I'm grateful that I still have my child and that she wasn't taken from me by people confusing poverty for neglect. I get nothing but compliments as to what a treasure she is. They were right.

I'm grateful for the ER doctor who admitted me to the hospital without a cent in order to evaluate my painful neurological condition which was weakening my legs.

I'm grateful for the isolation which provided me the chance to remove myself from the influence of others. Last but not least, an intense turning point: the birth of my daughter many years ago—the birth of a gorgeous baby girl who has brought great joy. My child had an excellent education. Now she still has excellence, but in an alternative form. But the greatest joy of all for me is being surrounded by breathtaking nature. There isn't a more beautiful place on the planet and I want to stay here forever.

Short Story for the Homeless: Baby owl. We were coming into town along the lakeshore and traffic was at a standstill, literally a standstill for miles. I checked for safety and got out. He was bewildered and sitting on the center line. I picked him up. He was no bigger than the size of a softball. I swear I could see a little smile on his face. The onlookers broke into a loud and enthusiastic applause from their cars. I opened my car door and he fluttered to the window and then hopped right onto the steering wheel. It felt like the energy of pure innocence. I am nothing if I can't bring us to a new home intact. So much of my spiritual health is at stake. But for now, what to do about the baby owl? Just then he startled us by flying out the window and up into nearby tall trees. I can't believe it happened. We worked it out. I'm sure he was back with his mother.

Mrs. Dundee once said she was embarrassed by her own riches. "You are a million times happier than I," she told me, "even with homelessness distracting you from so much of the rest of your life. How much caring do we have in us? Where do you draw the line for how much you care about life?"

Personally I don't think we can care too much, which is good because a few days later we came across another opportunity to serve our native wildlife.

Short story for the homeless: A full parade of baby painted turtles, obviously just hatched, swarming the road at the bottom of the hill, many of them already flattened. They were about the size of a nickel. The road had been built right down the middle of the marsh near where they laid their eggs. On either side of the road, houses were being built. Huge riding tractor mowers bowled over the ones in the grass. Most had no way out. After consulting with a naturalist about laws protecting wildlife and getting her input on how to pull this off, we put them in our backpack to transport them home where they could be placed in a temporary aquarium overnight. They seemed to be calmed by being in the pack. Like they somehow they knew that we humans were there to help them.

We met the naturalist at the state park the next day and released them under a small walking bridge. We stretched out on our stomachs in order to witness their safe release and share in their joy. The water was about five feet deep and crystal clear, about as close to God's protection as is possible. We could see each grain of sand at the bottom, the water was that clear, and watched as the tiny turtles glided up and down from deep to shallow.

Guilt. We all have it. It's everywhere. It surrounds us. If you have it, it needs to be taken care of. If not, I hope you have an active conscience.

We lost our home due to domestic abuse. I'd rather camp in the snow than live where it is not safe. My child was born into a turning point and has been turning ever since. I have turned away from violence and meanness and I will keep on turning. I refuse to give up my passions: children, the natural world and its wildness, its animals and all creatures. And don't ever forget: Great are the rewards for those who protect the innocent.

Amanda Lewis Having been trained in a range of both traditional and non-traditional therapies, Amanda began writing in hopes of shedding some light on a complicated subject, offering some meaningful and thoughtful solutions and not just the problems presented in so many stories today. After being encouraged by family and friends, Amanda set out to tell the story of "every woman" and therefore "every man" as well, and so her novel *Riding the Storm* was born. Amanda lives with her family in the upper Midwest and is working on her next two books.

Juan Linares

Growing Dreams and Marketing Hope

Moving to the Twin Cities from Mexico put me in the perfect position to help other Latinos in Minnesota get out of low-paying jobs by establishing business and integrating themselves into the local economy. Since the 1990s I've been involved in the revitalization of the East Lake Street corridor and especially in the creation of the Cooperative Mercado Central at Lake and Bloomington in Minneapolis—the first Latino coop. I also helped with organizing Plaza Latina on Payne Avenue on St Paul's East Side. Here's the story of how this came about.

When I came to the United States, I was clueless. I didn't speak more than a few words of English. It took me six months to feel comfortable even opening my mouth. I came to Minnesota with my wife nearly forty years ago. Because I had a green card, I didn't have any legal barriers to deal with, but I did have to understand the system, go to the social services, get to know people. And find a job.

I finally figured out the social services system, but what I wanted was a job. I was a business graduate from a Mexican university and thought I'd have great opportunities. Not so simple. I waited tables and worked at hotels. I managed a Burger King for a year.

Then I started working with Catholic Charities. They needed a bilingual service coordinator. I worked with them twenty-five years. The last ten years with them I did Latino outreach. I asked them to do it because of the amnesty granted under Reagan in 1986. I began helping all these newly legalized immigrants become part of the culture and economy.

Then welfare reform happened. We had been helping people with services, assistance, finding apartments and jobs, but I knew a lot of them were going to lose assistance and face becoming homeless when welfare was cut because they had such low-paying jobs—cleaning, hospitality, meatpacking, seasonal work in agriculture. So I began managing drop-in centers (daytime shelters) where we provided meals and social services such as job referrals, transitional housing, clothing, furniture, financial assistance, and advice on a daily basis.

But at the end of the day I was always faced with the question: Are we really helping people? There were bigger issues than just giving someone a dollar for the bus. A colleague challenged me saying, "You've got to get out of only looking at needs and begin to confront people. Find out what it is they want to do here."

People migrate to the United States from Latin America for economic reasons. They have hopes and dreams of a better life for their kids—education, a trade or a profession. What makes economic sense, then, is to give them opportunities to create things that work, to create measurable success. The way to do that is by discovering community members' own interests and vision. By exploring that, building relationships, giving folks the opportunity to excel, and showing them that success is not dependent on schooling, it's possible to create opportunities.

They all have a skill, a talent, maybe to sell, cook, run a restaurant. All of this benefits the community. It makes economic sense to encourage this creation of businesses. Then money circulates among ourselves five, six, seven times. It's good for the local economy. We show we can support ourselves. There's less dependency on federal dollars. That's healthy! It doesn't make economic sense to pay taxes and pour money into communities that remain poor and have crime. But when you give opportunities to people to be part of the solution, things change.

My colleague's comment really agitated me. I realized I didn't want to work at the level of hand-outs any more. Immigrants have so much to offer. They want to be part of the community in a meaningful way. But we needed organizing. So I went to the Gamaliel Foundation, a leadership training institute that works through faith-based communities. After that, we started Sagrado Corazón parish in Minneapolis in 1991. I met the pastor of a local Catholic church and asked him, "Would you be willing to open your doors to our Latino community?"

"What is it going to take?"

"Doing the service in Spanish."

"I don't speak Spanish."

"There are pastors who do," I told him. We contacted the Office of Hispanic Ministry of the St. Paul Archdiocese, and we began to organize around that religious service. Once we had a place, a sanctuary space, the community grew. They had a place where they could send their kids for catechism, and where they could come for other services that the church offers.

Through the church we formed a more meaningful and powerful Hispanic ministry. Soon other churches took an interest. I did the community part—the organizing and training. The pastors did the spiritual part. That's how we got started.

Organizing through faith-based communities gives people a space to start to understand how they can act in public life. We see how we can, in the name of social justice, reclaim or at least begin to challenge what is not just. We build community from the inside out. We explored our community's assets by doing a talent and capital inventory. This is an important tool. It tells us who we are and what we have. When we did the inventory at Sagrado Corazón, we saw we had people who were interested in starting their own businesses. This was the core group for the Cooperative Mercado Central.

Creating the Mercado Central took three years and involved a lot of committed people, a coalition of various organizations, and especially the Project for Pride in Living (PPL) to recondition three old warehouses. It was inaugurated in 1999 and has impacted commercial development in the area along Lake Street in Minneapolis. Before the migration to the suburbs, Lake Street was a bustling commercial area, but over decades of slow abandonment and flight to the suburbs, it became ridden with prostitution, drugs, and crime.

The Mercado served as an anchor in a severely challenged urban area. Its presence with some thirty to forty small businesses not only met the needs of the Latino community but brought other businesses to the area and brought the area back to life. It is also serves as a small business incubator and cultural center for the Latino community.

The development of Plaza Latina on the East side of St. Paul had its own trajectory. Once again we started with a church community in St. Paul. Our community was growing significantly in terms of participation and numbers, and they asked me, "Why can't we have a Mercado Central?" So we did the abilities and skills inventory and found out people were very serious about having a development in their St. Paul neighborhood. This was in 2002. We had an economic summit. Thirty-five people participated. We did the training—classes on starting a business, writing a business plan, leadership—and implemented the plan. The East Side Neighborhood Development Company partnered with the leadership of the Latino church community to bring this about.

Plaza Latina was an easier project than the Mercado Central and became a reality within a year. It's an association rather than a cooperative and, for the time being, they are renting the building. The late Senator Paul Wellstone spoke at the inauguration of Plaza Latina. This project has really had an impact on the neighborhood in the years it's been here. Other immigrant-owned businesses have now come into the area.

It feels really good to have helped in creating jobs and opportunities for people. Now they can buy homes, for example. That's an asset they will pass on to their kids. It's a way for families to build wealth. Immigrants have to be looked at as assets. One of the lessons I've learned is that you engage people by not just helping them develop their own capacities to grow and do what they are good at, but by letting them be the main agents of change. It's in their best interest to do that.

My commitment to helping establish the Latino business community here is motivated by an idea of justice, but it's also really a commitment to my relationships with people, to the individuals who in their turn commit to learning, growing, and taking on the responsibilities of business ventures. I try to engage each person and encourage, empower, and embolden him or her.

After these two successful projects, I worked with a foundation whose mission is reducing poverty in communities in eight states. I was asked to work with Latino communities applying the lessons learned from the Mercado Central and Plaza Latina.

"Forget we have any money," I'd tell the participants I was sent to work with. "How would you do this in your community? What do you want to achieve?" Folks started talking about how they would want to do it. The next step was to tap into their interests, intentionally build relationships, and help them become who they are and help individuals to become their own agents of change. People are afraid to come out of anonymity, to stop being invisible people. This is easier said than done and there are no short cuts to this. The first lesson is to help individuals see themselves as the leaders, as the producers of this change. Otherwise it's just providing social services.

I did the first step with them, and now they are in the process of implementing this work. From what I hear that is being done. But I left the foundation in spring of 2005 because this is not a prescription process. It's about building communities from the inside. To build powerful communities, you have to begin by building relationships in the community around self-interest and increase the relationships through networks. When I began my work, I organized one at a time. That's how we started the church, the Mercado, and the Plaza. That's how you help people recognize that they have what it takes to be the producers producing change, producing their own communities. I have to engage folks by building intentional, trusting relationships.

When I went to Idaho working for an organization, the first thing people saw was the checkbook. The foundation has money and people were saying what they thought we wanted to hear. But as it turned out, my way of promoting social change was not the foundation's way. We had a conflict of philosophies. I compromised for two years, but I wasn't willing to continue. We couldn't get into working with the undocumented. No one was going to challenge the institution. It wasn't in the foundation's self-interest. They just wanted to be recognized for their idea to end poverty.

Immigrants and immigration policy are never far from the spotlight or heated debates and wall-building proposals to keep out or throw out illegal immigrants. Immigrants contribute taxes. They are subsidizing public services and social security. And in return we're told we are criminals. We're told "You don't belong here." We have to recognize what we can contribute. We build tangible assets that keep us moving forward. Immigrants have to be looked at as assets.

We need to be more aware of the dangers of not understanding the complexity of immigration and how it affects people in their daily lives. I'm on the ground level in contact with people. To the fear that people express to me, I say, "Be calm, don't panic." We don't want people to leave. I tell folks, "Stay put, stay calm." But how can we continue our forward momentum if we are under attack? This makes my job more challenging—providing help and guidance to keep people from panicking. We can lose too much.

Yes, immigration law needs reform, but anti-immigrant sentiments cause fear and raise the possibility of grim scenarios. If people abandon their shops and businesses because of tougher, more exclusive immigration laws, what's the gain—the return of empty buildings on a desolate Lake Street or on any now thriving commercial corridor?

Juan Linares I continue working to promote, support and challenge the Latino community and its business members to grow and expand their vision in order to impact and even reshape the evolving political narrative. Currently I am assisting the Cooperative Mercado Central in Minneapolis as it transitions to total ownership of the property.

Philip Lund

A Persistent Echo

My heart is moved by all I cannot save:
So much has been destroyed
I have to cast my lot with those
who age after age, perversely,
with no extraordinary power,
reconstitute the world.

– Adrienne Rich

Not yet twenty, with a youthful self-confidence and the
relishing of adventure, I undertook an enlightening journey to
the East. Hungering to learn more about the world's
underpinnings, to witness all of its beauty and ugliness—and to
overcome my own naiveté, I knew I had to find my place in it.
If I were to contribute, it would be because I was capable of

deep understanding, tempered by firsthand experience, by the will to know, by the endurance of hardship.

This is my story, a telling of my journey. It is one of awakening, one of questioning. It is as much about gaining the strength to constantly overcome adversity as it is about the will to shape things—to become the earth's guardian. It is about the realization of the need to act, to play a part.

Deep down in my agitated soul there is a calm place, an oasis from the anguish, the turmoil, the senselessness of an often barbaric world, where I find the strength to endure and come to rest in an unwavering place of peace. There is a steadfast echo that I call upon, one that resounds so deeply that it enables me to persist in the face of difficult odds. It has provided with me with courage, a positive outlook and constant joy. I see no recourse but to work toward bettering life on this planet, where our humanity can prove itself, where our better natures can shape our communities, and where I might focus less on the cruelty everywhere—and less on the deep distress I experience as I witness injustice done to others.

This soul—this awakening consciousness—became enlivened rather early on. In my idyllic childhood with its meager beginnings, I played in the wheat fields, the sand pit, and among the cattails along the desolate shores of Lake Muskego, in southern Wisconsin. My days were spent barefoot, chasing leopard salamanders through the grass and following fish in the streams. I climbed walnut trees and built forts out of fallen branches, shagbark, rhubarb leaves and cornstalks. Such a serene world it was, free from outside harm.

As I grew and went to school, my field of vision widened. I was an impressionable child, easily awed by the sound of a flute, by our ability to harness electricity, by our human capability to run the 4-minute mile. I marveled at the skill of actors who can mimic others, of scientists who can predict outcomes, of painters who can create fine works of art, and at an unbounded future. I saw a hopeful time ahead for humanity and for myself.

To me, at the age of eleven, in the mid-1960s, it seemed like we were living at a time and place that was most assuredly civilized. I felt lucky, proud to be American, part of something quite advanced. And yet, big things were creeping into my consciousness, things that seemed incongruous with my life's view. I did not understand the inner workings of the Cuban Missile Crisis, could not fathom the assassination of President Kennedy and was confused by the Cold War. How could it be, in the twentieth century, in such a civilized society, that I had to practice ducking under my desk, in case—just in case—we were attacked by air? Was my desk a shelter from the world at large, or was our ducking a kind of stopgap solution to our problems—problems created by those in power. I thought then that there was something absurd about these air-raid drills, given our amazing capacities. I feel the same now about the weaker and more ignorant part of our natures. How could there be such forces, in modern times, such errant forces, where we still use violent solutions to settle differences, when we are capable of so much more?

It seems a natural progression that my early awareness would lead to even more troubling glimpses of large-scale violence. Notwithstanding an eagerness to learn, film footage left me wounded in the process. Horrific images of the concentration camps, of the chambers, of the body piles, were burned deeply into my core. How could an advanced society be responsible for the destruction of Hiroshima and Nagasaki? At a young age, America had failed me. My burgeoning sensitivity to our nation's history of lynchings, of church burnings, of the ruthless KKK, caused such internal angst. "Who are we?" The civil rights movement made so much sense. It was so long overdue.

As I entered high school in the 1960s, I studied poverty, overpopulation, and mobilized friends to get involved in the environmental movement. How could we be spoiling our waters and our air? It seemed that these were places where I could begin, where I might create a conversation, where things needed shaping. Before running and walking fundraisers were commonplace, I joined a planning committee in Madison, Wisconsin, to create the second Walk for Development. The first had been held in San Francisco. Substantial money was raised and used to teach farming techniques in the poverty-stricken communities of Biloxi, Mississippi and Chad, Africa. Shortly after, I became part of a contingent of planners at Madison area high schools to help spearhead the nation-wide Earth Day campaign, formulated by Wisconsin's Senator Gaylord Nelson to raise environmental awareness.

The world was coming forward, in purposeful ways, and I craved to see more of it. I had a zeal for life and held the belief that by exposing myself to other cultures, languages and customs, I would gain a more global perspective and in some way become wiser. At eighteen, I set out for my sophomore year of college in Copenhagen, Denmark. I made forays to the Soviet Union, communist East Germany and many parts of Europe. After that year, my lust for travel remained, and so I worked at a beer hall, in the vineyards of southern France, saved money, and made preparations to keep traveling. My next adventure would be a more grueling one. I set about on a long overland journey to India and Nepal. I knew the world was changing and that places like Yugoslavia, Afghanistan and Pakistan would not remain the same. How prophetic that all seems now. How fortunate I was to see that part of the world then.

It was on this trip that I discovered a force deep inside of me, a force that resonates now. This discovery imbued me with an energy that I possess today and that I rely upon when struggles seem insurmountable. It was during these travels in 1973, on a treacherous winter train ride through eastern Turkey, that I came upon this personal revelation. It unfolded while I was on the move, heading toward Tehran, Iran. After frigid weeks of making my way through much of the Eastern European Bloc, I was still carrying residual tension with me. I had just witnessed the terrible oppressiveness suffered by the many people living under communist rule. My awakening to the crushing power of military authority, the ever-present secret police, and the unjust restraints, raised my appreciation for basic human rights. While feeling profoundly lucky to be free, the winter conditions were reminding me of my own vulnerability.

Though the cold and rugged train ride was most unpleasant, I remained open to the idea that this journey to the east would be a spiritual one. My recent experiences were heightening my awareness. As my traveling partner and I approached the Iranian border on rough rails, at a sluggish pace, over an icy expansive lake, the temperature plummeted to well below freezing. The landscape was a desolate one. Due to overcrowded conditions in the train compartments, we were forced into the unheated aisle for what seemed to be an eternity. Darkness and dangerous conditions had long set in, the floor was encrusted in ice, and there was little chance of gaining sleep. I slipped into a torpid state leaning against a wall. I awoke falling backwards, then scratched away the crystals from a frosted window to see beyond. At this moment, as I was pushing through discomfort, I felt deeply alive. This was a cathartic occurrence, an anagnorisis, a critical moment of self-discovery. I was young and learning that I had to stand alone against difficult outside forces. This was the thickening of empowerment.

Just days before, while in a poetic state of mind, I had told myself that during this trip I would search for the lost chord— that one resonant force which would overtake my being and forever mold my character. I was searching for something, some internal driving force that could propel me forward, provide meaning and purpose and give me a sense of direction. At the root of my search I discovered an inner strength, a well-source of energy which I could trust. I acquired a kind of courage and came to know my deep ability to endure. The chord was struck.

The power of finding this lost chord is well described in the following poem by Adelaide Anne Proctor. Written in 1858, it reflects the work of this philanthropist who dedicated her short life to issues of homelessness, poverty and women's rights.

The Lost Chord

Seated one day at the organ,
I was weary and ill at ease,
And my fingers wandered idly
Over the noisy keys.

I do not know what I was playing,
Or what I was dreaming then;
But I struck one chord of music,
Like the sound of a great Amen.

It flooded the crimson twilight,
Like the close of an Angel's Psalm,
And it lay on my fevered spirit
With a touch of infinite calm.

It quieted pain and sorrow,
Like love overcoming strife;
It seemed the harmonious echo
From our discordant life.

It linked all perplexed meanings
Into one perfect peace,
And trembled away into silence
As if it were loth to cease....

This poem hangs with me, and on occasion it reminds me of my journey.

Days after the train ride, while moving through the vast desert plain of southeastern Iran, I was keenly aware of the risks we were taking, and I was feeling deeply alive again. I ventured alone away from our safari vehicle, wondering about its trustworthiness, traversed to the other side of an immense scorched dune, and scratched a message in the sand. I knew full well that the wind would quickly erase my words and that my drifting signature would matter not. I again became aware of my solitary presence, more than ever before. I have come to trust my inner voice, a voice that incessantly stands up for "what it is to be human." As humans we are moving toward an earth community, where resources need to be shared, differences need to be celebrated, and violence needs be reduced. These are the traits of an advancing species.

Today, I work toward progress and I often reflect upon that trip and the early lessons learned.

In India, I became aware of severe contrasts, contrasts that seem unfair. On a sidewalk in Bombay, now Mumbai, I watched a bejeweled woman walking, wrapped in a beautiful sari, and side-by-side, a one-armed, one-legged man, on a makeshift cart, begging as he pushed his way along. Such disparity exists in our world. It must be examined. Obstacles that cause inequality must be considered and overcome. Discontent and inequality often lead to violence. It is in our understanding of violence, in our study of it that we see below the aggression—we see human needs. We come to know why healthy minds and bodies make a difference, why the protection of our natural resources are important, why equal access to food and water matter, why shelter and safety are essential, and why we search for purpose and meaning. I presently serve as the facilitator for the Peace and Social Justice Writers Group, at the Loft Literary Center, in Minneapolis, Minnesota. In this capacity, with the profound influence of the others in the group, we dig deep, uncover these contrasts, and search for the causes. We take risks in our discussions. As writers and activists, we consider our roles in society and share our unique experiences and views. We develop compassion, flex our intellectual grasp, internalize the lessons learned, and each of us, in our own way, actualizes an inner peace—one we are compelled to share in our outside conversations and in our daily work.

In Turkey, I was confused by the steady stare of men's eyes and by the intimidating close-proximity of strangers talking to me, only to learn that such body language and positioning is part of that culture. In my architectural work I have called upon this experience. Not long ago, by studying human proxemics, the study of human spatial relationships, I used the knowledge gained to assist with the design of a treatment center for victims of torture. Survivors of torture lose trust in the closeness of others; therefore, the creation of healing spaces is essential for recovery, where natural light is present, colors are non-agitating, a safe exit is visible and furniture arrangements are non-threatening. According to a fairly recent report, Amnesty International estimates that at least 81 world governments currently practice torture, some of them openly. Healing work is necessary to overcome the deep pain caused by physical and psychological abuse. Healing is also necessary to mend the divisions caused by other forms of injustice, wrongs committed to whole populations throughout history. Pain leaves an imprint, one that lasts for generations.

In progressive voices there is a wisdom. I align myself with them. Forward thinking people articulate and advance the social, political, and environmental issues of their time. Human history is permeated with advancements that are defined by their age: the Age of Reason, the Enlightenment, the Renaissance, the Industrial Age, the Space Age, this Age of Technology. Perhaps now, due to all of these advances, civilization is asking that we put the human race in order, that we advance our interworkings, that we—using all of our previous forward movements in so many complex disciplines—come together in an Age of Human Understanding. We can work together to overcome our most complicated problems: terrorism, overpopulation, the lack of resources, the fouling of our planet, the rise of seemingly random acts of violence, the increase in suicide rates, the migration of peoples in search of work, the consumption of valuable capital to fuel unnecessary wars that maim the minds, hearts and spirits of soldiers.

Ages define themselves, as if there is something in the air, something contagious, where we are all formulating, all looking for answers at the same time. The answers to our current problems will not merely be found in the complex calculations of a Newton, in the beauty of a Michelangelo, in the teachings of a Christ, in the production lines of a Henry Ford. These are the most difficult answers of all, where technology alone, religion alone, interplanetary travel to colonize other habitable places alone cannot solve our most complex quandaries. We must opt for the highest ground possible. We must join our best minds with our deepest understandings. We must bridge differences and work together to overcome shortages: of energy, of water, of respect for order, of respect for each other, of respect for the planet.

It is in our working together, in our local communities, in our private conversations, as active agents, that we will shape a better future. Many peoples of the earth suffer from ethnic, religious, gender, economic and political oppression and from violence. Many bear the wounds of subjugation, of decades-long hardship and they struggle to the find a most basic sense of human dignity. There is reason for hope as many reach out to help, and as peacemakers are rapidly shaping the conversation.

Can I say that a single experience, that a long hard journey in my past was instrumental in forming my character, or that it causes me to work hard to help solve complex problems? Such a claim would overlook the significance of all the other forces at work in my single life. I cannot separate myself from what I see happening around me—my spirit and my heart are engaged. I am calmed by doing. I do know that I need to forge ahead. We need to forge ahead. Change comes neither easily, nor quickly. Work is needed to improve things. That I call upon my ability to persevere, that there is something that resonates deep in my soul, I have no doubt. That we need to persevere is without question.

Philip Lund—As an architect-builder at Philip J. Lund Design + Construction, Inc., Lund believes in the power of relationships to improve lives, communities and the environment. In 2009, he created an outdoor science classroom for a local middle school. This amphitheater, built out of flattop boulders, in a natural hillside bowl, was a no-waste initiative. For Nonviolent Peaceforce, he helped stage the fundraising production of "A Peoples' History of the United States," with renowned activist Howard Zinn as the host. Nonviolent Peaceforce is an international peacekeeping effort that uses unarmed, non-partisan teams trained in conflict resolution to overcome violence around the world. As the facilitator for the Peace and Social Justice Writers Group, Lund is its delegate to the Minnesota Alliance of Peacemakers, a 75-member organization that works to strengthen the regional peace and justice community. He recently served as a judge and host for its first annual, statewide peace essay contest for high school juniors and seniors. As a community organizer, he serves as the Treasurer and Giving Program Director for the Golden Valley Community Foundation and is currently working on an initiative that is conducting community dialogues to support diversity in the higher ranks of local government. As board member of the local farmers market and planning team member for the local arts and music festival, he believes that vibrant communities are supported by healthy living, intellectual exchange, and by people working together.

Rose McGee

Sweet Potato Comfort Pie Power—
Eyes On the Pie!

Awh shake it to the east! Awh shake it to the west! Awh shake it to the one that you love the best! As a little girl, I was actively engaged in various story circle games that not only had each of us talking, listening, giggling or crying, but often had us communicating with energetic movements of stomping, clapping, jumping or whatever seemed fitting for the moment. A great example was *Little Sally Walker*. During recess at school, all of us girls would be in circle, chanting the repetitive lyrics that required acting out the song's instructions. Needless to say there were always a few of boys who wanted to get into the mix. How they had treated us in the classroom or on the school bus ride would determine whether we allowed them to join in our games—generally NOT.

The song was all about *Little Sally Walker* who was sitting in a saucer. One of us would start by sitting in the middle of the circle as *Sally* until told by our chanters to *"Rise Sally rise!*

Wipe your weeping eyes, put your hands on your hips and let your hips and let your backbone slip. Awh shake it to the east! Awh shake it to the west! Awh shake it to the one that you love the best!" (That's probably why those silly boys wanted to be in our circle game.) Meanwhile, whoever *Sally* pointed to became the next *Sally*. Then the chosen one would enter into the center of the *circle* and proceed to carry out the routine as before.

We would play that little game over and over for hours it seemed. After all, everyone was to have a chance at being Sally. When our individual turn came up, the manner in which we exhibited our movement was our very *own* story...and it sure said a lot about our personalities. Some of the girls hardly moved a muscle due to shyness or the feeling of having embarrassingly less than others to actually shake, while some of us early developers shook *it* to the east and shook *it* to the west with absolutely all our might!

Reverentially, I welcome recounting such innocent childhood memories for that's when the seeds of character values were being planted. Little did I know that an inner strength of *shaking with all my might* was taking deep roots to later fortify me for magnanimous climbs up countless and horrendous mountains of womanhood. There would be many times ahead, especially at night, when I would cry in the privacy of my bedroom because during the day, I refused to display any signs of defeat. Absolutely not!

Since church had been a regular routine since birth, I knew how to pray anytime, anywhere. My cries were for strength to navigate up those mountains by shaking off discouragement, racism, sexism, being a single mom after two failed marriages, being invisible in the workplace, death of my son, death of my husband, not to mention job layoff that led to housing foreclosure which totally ruined my credit. Had I not *acquired* power to shake off defeat at an early age, I would never have survived. By doing so, somewhere in the scheme of things, my eyes opened to an interesting call from reality...IT AIN'T ALL ABOUT YOU AND YOUR SURVIVAL!

That revelation prompted me into a response of inquiry…*Okay, I get it! I am not the only person in this world struggling or in pain, so what can I do to soothe others and encourage them to learn to shake with every ounce of strength in their being?*

I grew up in a rural community in Jackson, Tennessee, with my paternal grandmother and great-grandmother who we affectionately called Mama Rosie and Mom'Allie, respectively. When someone was in need of comfort, in a heartbeat those women would whip up a batch of sweet potato pies and deliver to the ailing or the mourning. Now, here's the thing…I was the light of these two women's eyes (and I loved it). There were no other grandchildren at the time because my father was an only child. When Dad finished his military duty with the United States Army, he moved to Minneapolis, Minnesota. Being a responsible father, he wanted to make sure that his child was properly taken care of, so I was left to be raised by these two women. My birthmother, young and immature, was a city girl from Gary, Indiana, and hated the South. When she and my father decided there would be no marriage between them, the only property settlement to be resolved was me. By the time I was nine months old, she totally agreed with Dad to place me with his mother. To Mama Rosie, it was the best decision my parents could have made. Since Mom'Allie also lived with her, the two women now had me to love and pamper while I had them to protect me from all harm. Though we were plain ole' country folks, we knew the abundance of life's natural richness…love.

Mama Rosie owned her own land, was the bread winner, and supported us by being a domestic helper for the local white women while Mom'Allie took care of our own home and, of course, me. Both women had been widowed for several years and knew how to take care of things just fine without having a man to run things for them. Besides, among all the uncles, nephews, and cousins there was always male strength around to handle repairs or heavy lifting. Although I had chores, I never had to cook. Other than church, the kitchen was Mom'Allie's sacred space. She found joy in preparing a heaping breakfast and a whopping supper. My duties were to chop up the onions, peel potatoes, collect whatever she needed from the garden out back and gather eggs from the henhouse while she turned those items into meals to die for. Ohhhhhh that woman could cook! There was always something in the kitchen such as a freshly cooked pot of mustard, turnip or collard greens, a skillet of buttered corn bread and better yet, a succulent sweet potato pie. That's probably why those male relatives were always eager to help around the house.

One day (I was no more than six or seven years old), Mom'Allie took me to visit one of our neighbors, Miss Mae. All of us neighborhood children were terrified of Miss Mae. After all, she was *different* from us. She looked scary and the woman never talked, just mumbled. When passing her house, we would cross over to the opposite side of the road for fear she would snatch us up and do whatever evil witches do with children… like in that story we'd heard about *Hansel and Gretel.* To us Miss Mae was some sort of witch for sure. Although none of us had ever been inside her house, we knew there was a giant pot sitting on a huge stove just waiting for little children to be put into and boiled. Truth be told, we were running off theories ignited only by our own imaginations.

It would be later in life before I would come to understand that Miss Mae was albino…thus the reason for her pale-white skin and pink eyes. And although she spoke inaudibly, she had the amazing ability to communicate with few people…the ones she trusted. How did I get to this point? Well…

One day Mom'Allie decided she was going to take a sweet potato pie to a friend. This was not unusual. Being her little darling, I often had the pleasure of accompanying her on these visits. She loved showing me off to her friends because "they said" I was like an *old spirit.* Made sense considering how much I hung around old women. Mom'Allie did not drive an automobile nor did she ever have much of a desire to ride in one, so she and I generally walked the graveled Pipkin Road where we lived and often took short cuts through the wooded trails. On this particular day, two sweet potato pies baking in the oven had the house smelling like heaven. As usual, one pie was for the house and I was always the designated taste-tester. Soon, my tummy was full from my usual generous slice. Plus, the rule in our house was, *never go to anyone else's house hungry.*

As we prepared to embark upon our journey, Mom'Allie wrapped the second pie with a dishcloth (there was no aluminum foil at that time). The real excitement for me was the journey along the way. Mom'Allie knew so much about everything—tree varieties, which herbs I could touch, which ones not to touch, the pretty birds, the wild flowers— everything! I would ask her loads of questions about this berry or that bug, and she knew all the answers. Without realizing it, time would have passed and we'd reached our destination of some old lady or another's house where the women would talk on and on about everything and everybody, it seemed.

Even at such a young age, my *old spirit* found it interesting listening to the stories they exchanged. However, since I was after all, only a child, often I would nap in between some of the "who got baptized last Sunday" or "who the District Conference was going to send to our country CME church to be the next pastor." So this particular day, I was excited about our adventure to whoever we were going to visit and take a pie.

OH NO! We were going to Miss Mae's house! I did not sign up for this trip! Being terrified was an understatement and I wanted to run back through the woods and down that graveled road back home. Mom'Allie told me to calm down and that there was nothing to be afraid of except my own shadow. Well, I certainly WAS NOT afraid of my own shadow, so very tightly I eased as close to Mom'Allie as I could get, then clamped my arms around one of her legs as we entered Miss Mae's one room, paintless, wooden-framed house. Mom'Allie greeted Miss Mae who gazed down at me with her pink eyes that looked more like two slits because they were so slanted, and handed Miss Mae the sweet potato pie.

With pie in hand, the tiny, delicate woman dashed across the room to a small wooden table that held a pile of items—a small tin pot, a cast-iron skillet, a few dishes, some match boxes, crackers, cans of food, a few eating utensils, and more. Underneath piles of stuff, she located a spoon and immediately dug into that pie as though it was the only food on earth. She took a bite, smiled, took another bite, and then another. Delightfully, she looked at Mom'Allie and also at me. That's when I could see she had no teeth. Before I could react from the shock of such a sight, even more baffling to me were the tears rolling down her thin, translucent cheeks.

Confused, by the exhibition of her emotions, I felt as though I was going to cry. *Witches don't cry do they?* Mom'Allie beckoned me to sit down next to her in one of the two wooden chairs positioned in the room. Miss Mae sat in a creaking rocking chair near us. As Miss Mae and Mom'Allie communicated in an odd fashion, the warmth of their exchange gradually lifted my fears. Wasn't long before Mom'Allie was waking me up from a nap.

After visiting Miss Mae that day, all the way home, I was very quiet and so was Mom'Allie. Every now and then she and I would exchange a glance or two, but for some reason, I was not up to asking questions about the plants or insects. From that day on, I was no longer frightened of Miss Mae. Matter of fact, on many occasions, I delivered jars of canned vegetables and food that Mom'Allie had prepared. My great-grandmother knew that I needed a lesson in understanding how to love all people. She demonstrated that act through something as simple as "sweet potato pie."

Almost two decades later, yet I remember the day very well, Sweet Potato Pie came *calling* on me. I was married and living in Denver, Colorado (a mighty long way from Tennessee). For some reason, I woke up early one Saturday morning with the desire to make a blackberry cobbler AND a sweet potato pie for Sunday dinner. I had no idea how to make either. Truth be told, my repertoire in the kitchen was still extremely limited. By now, Mom'Allie had passed away, so I did what was still the most natural thing. I called Mama Rosie and asked her for instructions. What happened next was my awakening. The blackberry cobbler was HORRIBLE and tasted like little rocks with no resemblance to berries. On the other hand, the sweet potato pie was really quite tasty and received lots of compliments which inspired me to make it more often. Before long, I was fairly good at it. But under no circumstances did my pie come close to tasting like Mom'Allie's or Mama Rosie's. I concluded years ago: *Can't nobody make a sweet potato pie like my two Mamas.*

Not to be a quitter, a few weeks later I tried my hand at making that blackberry cobbler again. It turned out worse than before. The message was clear—this dessert was NOT for me to make. People were now requesting me to make sweet potato pie for various gatherings. Yet, it would still be another thirty years before I would recognize and understand that Sweet Potato Pie and I had a mission together. Thirty years! I leaned into the power of this pie and saw it as being the *sacred* dessert of Black people, a catalyst for caring and building community. So how did I reach the inevitable?

On August 9, 2014...another bloody hot day. There I sat in the comfort of my air-conditioned home watching media coverage of another Black mother's son lying lifeless on a scorching asphalt street, this time in Ferguson, Missouri. Like others prior, the news of Michael Brown's death tore at my heart as I thought *that could have been my son.* I ached for the unknown mother who would never again hear a response to her call, "Come on inside, baby, it's time to eat!" And so I wept.

Escalating hotter than the weather was the tremendous tension from protesters. As I viewed eyes filled with anger and fear flash across my television screen, I asked myself, *what can I do?* There came a soft yet clear response (I believe from God). *Go into your kitchen, make some sweet potato pies, pack your car, and deliver them down to Ferguson.* And so I did.

Friday August 29, 2014, at the crack of dawn my son Adam and I hit the road with thirty freshly baked sweet potato pies in the trunk of my car. (Ironic that it would be thirty pies, since it took me thirty years to realize the power of this pie.) Meanwhile, my daughter and pastor, Roslyn created a poem to accompany each pie. Upon arrival, first, I *asked* permission of the person to accept a pie and soon discovered that each one had something to share about *how* the pie had come at just the right time. And so I listened.

The Ferguson stories sparked a deeper sense of urgency within me to do more. Commemorating the legacy of Reverend Doctor Marin Luther King, Jr., was the perfect start. In less than two months, in my community of Golden Valley, Minnesota I organized over fifty intergenerational and culturally diverse community volunteers to bake eighty-six pies. The number represented King's age had he been alive in 2015. People shared personal stories such as racial disparities, bullying, and celebrations from overcoming challenging situations. Among themselves, participants then decided who to award the pies to which included police departments, hospitals, school principals, politicians, individuals, and families. Lives became transformed by this pie.

The horror of June 17, 2015 was ringing in my ears in total disbelief. Thirteen African Americans were shot and nine killed senselessly by a young white man while the people were worshipping in church. Those murders left the members of Mother Emanuel AME Church and the citizens of Charleston, South Carolina in total devastation. People across the country were traumatized. My neighbor, Eden Bart and I delivered and served fifty-six sweet potato pies to Charleston.

Ferguson remained under watch as the one-year anniversary of Michael Brown's death was approaching and unrest was projected due to the denial of a community's request for justice. In November 2015, one week before Thanksgiving, as our Sweet Potato Comfort Pie Team was preparing to bake and deliver pies to Ferguson to promote peace, comfort, conversation, and community building, we were slammed with news that another young Black male, Jamar Clark, was shot and killed by a police officer here at home in one of our own communities. Instead of traveling to Ferguson, we needed to now focus on home. And then…

I felt an interesting nudge. This time, rather than just me leading a team of volunteers to bake pies, I called upon other local bakers to join in. As a result, six African-American-owned restaurants and caterers located in Minneapolis and Saint Paul baked pies. Altogether we created sixty sweet potato pies. Not only did we deliver the pies to the protest site of Precinct Four in north Minneapolis, but volunteers also carried pies to community leaders, police officers, and the Clark family.

Evil is such an ugly force. During this act of caring, at some point, it was rumored by a hate group that the pies were "injected with rat poison and all who ate them would die." Of course the pies were not poisoned; all were eaten and everyone remained healthy. On the other hand, sadly, within thirty-six hours after delivering the pies, three self-proclaimed white supremacists infiltrated the peaceful protest site and shot five unarmed people. Fortunately, none were killed. This call to action prompted an even greater outpouring of food as Black Lives Matters and NAACP continued to lead the standoff that lasted for two weeks. I am so mindful of Frederick Douglass: *Power concedes nothing without a demand. If there is no struggle there is no progress.*

Sweet Potato Comfort Pie is not just about race, although it is about race. I acknowledge "It's in the batter—Black lives do matter!" And I also acknowledge that "Beneath the peeling— it's the healing!" Minnesota Congressman Keith Ellison commented during our 2016 Martin Luther King, Jr., Sweet Potato Comfort Pie Day of Service: "There is much pain in America. If something as simple as a pie can bring people together and begin a dialogue that moves us forward in a positive way, then why not pie!" My dear friend Kate Towle said, "We have to keep our eyes on the pies, don't we Rose?" From that comment evolved our tag line, "Eyes on the Pies."

The history, the legacy, and the richness of Sweet Potato Pie's strengthening qualities keeps me grounded. Further inspiration is sparked by a phenomenal mover and determined shaker Mary McLeod Bethune, a child of former slaves, who grew up to be an educator determined to see other Black youth receive higher education. To raise money to do so, she often rode her bicycle selling sweet potato pies. That prestigious school is now Bethune Cookman University in Daytona Beach, Florida. Memories of Mama Rosie and Mom' Allie keep me focused on the gift of being humble enough to serve others. There is power in pie!

Rose McGee understands and respects the power of *sweet potato pie* mixed with authentic *storytelling* in *circle.* The combination is a catalyst for caring and building community in ways that impact human relations. Often referred to as "The Pie Lady," she is creator of the community initiative Sweet Potato Comfort Pie as well as being a professional storyteller, author, facilitator, and owner of Deep Roots Gourmet Desserts. She earned a Master's Degree in Education from Lesley University, Cambridge, Massachusetts.

By utilizing her own creative expertise, she works with Minnesota Humanities Center's Absent Narratives initiative by providing professional development designed to inspire educators, parents, and students. She is author of the play *Kumbayah The Juneteenth* Story, the video *Sleep With A Virgin A Perspective On AIDS,* and several poetry books. Rose is founder of the convening concepts: Headscarf Society™, TeaLit™, and co-author of the newly released book *Story Circle Stories.* She is a featured Tedx Talk presenter on "The Power of Pie" where she tells why sweet potato pie is the sacred dessert of Black culture.

Rose's award-winning sweet potato pie was a guest of Minnesota Senator Amy Klobuchar in Washington D.C. during the 2008 Inauguration of President Obama that featured ten Minnesota foods. In addition to numerous pie demonstrations, national television/radio interviews, and news articles, in August 2015 she was featured in the National Public Broadcasting Station documentary: *A Few Good Pie Places.* Rose personally delivered and served fifty-six sweet potato pies to members of Mother Emanuel

AME Church in Charleston, South Carolina where nine people were killed while worshiping. She is a member of Women Who Really Cook, is a recipient of the 2015 Minnesota Social Impact Center Change-Maker Award, Bush Foundation's BushConn Award, Golden Valley Community Foundation Sparks Grant, and the Calvary Lutheran Church (Golden Valley) Fellowship Grant.

Paul Mayer

A Monk in the Civil Rights Movement: Encounter with Dr. Martin Luther King, Jr.

It was on the morning of March 7, 1965 that Dr. Martin Luther King, Jr. sent out an emergency call from Selma, Alabama, for clergy and religious people to join him there in the critical struggle for voting rights for Black people. Early that morning, over five hundred activists, including the leaders of the voters' rights campaign, had been brutalized by the billy clubs, bullwhips, rubber tubing wrapped in barbed wire, tear gas and horses of the Alabama State Police and Highway Patrol. The police attacked the little band as it attempted to march nonviolently across the Pettus Bridge, which spanned the Chattahoochee River in Selma.

It was then that Dr. King made the simple, almost brutal calculation that the time had come for the white churches and synagogues to put it on the line, even if that meant some white clergy skulls might get cracked and bloodied. He had written in his Letter from Birmingham City Jail that the clergy had "too often been the taillight rather that the headlight" of the struggle for justice.

Now King was stricken with remorse because a preaching commitment in his Atlanta church had prevented his own presence in Selma on that morning. Hence the passion and outrage in his call for "a ministers' march to Montgomery":

"In the vicious treatment of the defenseless citizens of Selma, where old women and young children were gassed and clubbed at random, we have witnessed an eruption of the disease of racism which seeks to destroy all America. The people of Selma will struggle on for the soul of America, but it is fitting that all Americans help bear the burden."

This emergency call from Selma came to my attention at dawn on Monday, March 8, in a radio bulletin, shortly after the daily morning Mass sung by our community of monks in the ancient Gregorian chant in our peaceful abbey in New Jersey. Mass that day was on Monday of the first week of Lent and the day's Scripture readings were stunningly appropriate:

"I will look for those which are lost and bring back those which have strayed, and I will bind up any crippled one, and I will make the weak one strong…and I will feed them in justice. "(Ezekiel 34:15)

"Then these in their turn will ask Him: 'Lord, when did we see You hungry or thirsty, a stranger or naked, sick or in prison and did not come to Your help?' Then He will answer them: 'Of a truth I tell you, in so far as you did not do this to one of these least ones, you did not do it to Me.'" (Matthew 25:44-45)

My strong lifelong feelings about justice for Black people began with my family's close bond with Ethel Benjamin, our African-American cleaning lady, one of the noblest souls I will ever know. In her quiet, dignified way she had shared with me the bitter reality of her family's life in Harlem. More recently Thomas Merton's unsparing "Letter to a White Liberal" had further fueled this passion.

So on that Monday morning, it became absolutely clear to me that I must answer the urgent summons issued by Dr. King. Yet the likelihood of receiving permission from my Abbot seemed extremely slim. He had already once denied me permission to attend a simple ecumenical peace retreat.

Nevertheless, I determinedly decided to find a way. My first step was to confer with Father Aloysius, the only Black monk of our community (we said "Negro" in those days). Father Aloysius was an altogether delightful character. His skin color was deep brown and he looked very much like an African teacher rather than someone from this continent. Of slight build and medium height, his most striking characteristic was his deep brown eyes made even larger behind thick rimless glasses. Slightly bowed, Father Aloysius (or Allie) was the consummate scholar, always immersed in a theological tome.

He had entered the Abbey a few years behind me and we had struck it off right away as the local minorities on the block. Behind his quiet, scholarly demeanor there burned a profound commitment to justice. We often commiserated and joked together about the state of the world, the church and of our own monastery. It must have been incredibly difficult to be the only Black in this all-white world, a feeling I often shared, although there was one other Jewish monk, Father Ambrose. It was always surprising to see Father Aloysius flame out from behind his reserved demeanor when something touched his heart.

He immediately responded with intense enthusiasm to my proposal. Needless to say, he shared my profound skepticism about receiving permission from our superiors, but we were determined that the ancient Benedictine motto of PAX would be more than the traditional inscription over the monastery gate.

This would truly be an enterprise guided by the Spirit. The first indication of this providential guidance was the news that Father Abbot Charles was away on a prolonged trip. The Abbot's absence, however, did not necessarily mean our trip was a "shoo in," since we would now have to deal with the Prior, the next in command. He and I had experienced some run-ins over my pacifist views on war and nonviolence, which ran counter to his Marine background. He seemed to regard me as something of a loose cannon and generally as an exponent of the latest dangerous naïve idea on either church or state. Hence it must have been through some angelically inspired lapse of memory or perhaps some thus far unsuspected sympathy with the civil rights cause that the Prior granted us permission to go.

Neither Father Aloysius nor I could quite believe our ears. We hastily threw a few things into a bag and changed from our monastic habits into the musty black suits and stiff white Roman collars which were reserved for those rare and dangerous sojourns into what was then known to us as "the world." Our flight from Newark to Montgomery was an adventure in the early 1960s, since air travel was not common, especially for the likes of us.

Some young Black organizers from the Southern Christian Leadership Conference (SCLC) were not the only ones to greet us at the Montgomery Airport. The local Catholic archbishop had stationed a few of his imported Irish priests to discourage any priests and nuns in collar and habit from joining the campaign in Selma. After all, Dr. King had been accused of being a Communist, a defamation inspired by the smear campaign of FBI Director, J. Edgar Hoover. "Sure, Father, and you'd best be returning back home right away. The Bishop is warning priests and religious not to get involved in dangerous politics here." All this was not surprising since the Bishop had a well-earned reputation for his thunderous silence on segregation in his diocese. Needless to say, we politely but determinedly ignored this episcopal prohibition and piled into the rickety old jalopies that would transport us to Selma and one of the most transformative experiences of our lives.

Within a matter of hours, we had been catapulted from the peace and seclusion of our rural monastic solitude into the heat of the civil rights struggle at one of its most historically intense moments. Added to that was the fact that I had never been in the South before and was experiencing culture shock on many levels.

Above all, I experienced intense feelings of euphoria and excitement, and perhaps even a little apprehension. I was deeply moved at the thought of being in the very center of a reality that I had only thought and read about, and in some inner way involved myself in for years—the fight for racial justice in America. It was also the first time that I had been transported from an all-white world into this human mass of predominantly Black folk who were even (presumptuously, it seemed to my still uneducated and somewhat racist consciousness) in the leadership of this movement and making key decisions for all of us.

Here I was in my black suit and clerical Roman collar, my short haircut, still young and inexperienced and wet behind the ears at the age of thirty-four, suddenly surrounded by all of this intensity and life. There was a powerful charge to all this political passion, all this fierce struggle against the status quo, all of this close community, all of this proximity to shared danger and even death which generated unspoken feelings of terror. People were being attacked and even killed.

The religious people who arrived in response to Dr. King's emergency call were housed with members of the local Black community. It was Aloysius' and my good fortune to be received by the Simpson family into their modest whitewashed little house. They were an older couple and showered us with simple warm Southern hospitality and treated us like honored guests. They seemed amazed that all these Northerners, especially white people, would come to support them. Little did they realize (and much less ourselves) that it was we who would be enriched beyond our wildest dreams by this experience.

It came as a shock, like a hammer blow to the temple, to realize how poor these generous people were. I could hardly believe my eyes when I opened the refrigerator door looking for a cold drink to discover there one solitary container of milk. It began to dawn on me that my religious vow of poverty was more like a well-intentioned pious charade when compared to the lives of poor Black men and women here and in other parts of the world. This lone container of milk would come to represent the awakening of a new level of consciousness that would stay with me in a haunting way. It shattered the myth of self-satisfied virtue and Liberal commitment. It overwhelmed me with a sense of my own privilege and safety in the face of the majority of the people of the world who survived at the edge of misery and existential uncertainty about the next day, the next moment. The memory of this container of milk began the reluctant process of education that would follow me into the barrios of Central America and into the despair of our own urban ghettos and Indian reservations.

Nor was I prepared for the fearsome intensity of the racial hatred which was the lifeblood of the ugly system of segregation and which we had presumptuously come to challenge. It was more than difficult to maintain the biblical perspective of loving one's enemies and turning the other cheek. This would be one of the many lessons that I was to learn from the community of poor and simple "uneducated" people who lived under the terror of this culture of racial segregation and would continue to do so long after we returned to the safety of our white religious institutions.

I can still feel—and almost taste—the bitter animosity and rancor of local whites toward us, since most of us were easily identifiable as the classical Yankee outside agitators. The very fact of Blacks and whites working together to destroy their way of life was an affront and a threatening provocation.

The local and state police represented these attitudes under the guise of law enforcement. It is still hard to imagine how these "peace officers" felt fully justified in treating the Black community with contempt, hatred and brutality. But it was clear that these same attitudes and policies were to apply to "nigger lovers" and other kinds of troublemakers like ourselves.

It was always unsettling to see John Daws of the U.S. Justice Department and a slew of FBI agents consorting and joking with the state and local police. These included County Sheriff Jim Clark, who enjoyed a well-deserved reputation as a racist bigot and was infuriated by this uppity multicolored resistance movement.

It was truly the Spirit guiding and inspiring this movement as it confronted the ancient institutions and ways of thinking so deeply rooted in the evils of chattel slavery. Nothing brought this home to me like the nightly gatherings in Selma's Brown Chapel. The "chapel" was actually a good-sized brick structure with striking Romanesque towers which had originally been built by freedmen after the Civil War and now served as headquarters for this freedom movement.

On one of my first nights after the Freedom Rally, I sat towards the front of the sanctuary with Viola Liuzzo, a white woman from Detroit. As we talked she quietly told me why she had left her family to represent the Unitarian community in this historic campaign for freedom. One of their own ministers, Rev. James Reeb, had been clubbed to death a few weeks earlier. I was impressed by her simple modesty in describing her commitment.

These gatherings were a combination of prayer services, extraordinary community gospel singing, and spirit rallies to empower us for the freedom struggle of the next day with its threats and potential of violence, beatings and perhaps even death.

Here was a vibrant form of religiosity, radically different from my past experience. It resembled neither the Jewish rituals of my childhood nor the solemn liturgy of Benedictine monasticism. It was completely new and unfamiliar. This was worship that was warm and alive, traditional and yet spontaneous. It integrated the call and response of slave field songs into memories of ancient African traditional religions. Everybody seemed part of the experience, seemed to own it, even to the point of answering back to the preacher. The prayers came from the heart and the preaching (because the "movement" talks were really preaching) was emotional, loud and often outrageous.

Above all, the music called forth in me a deep feeling of coming home. When the community sang, "I'm Gonna Eat at the Welcome Table," tears welled up from deep within me. When the charismatic Reverend James Bevel spoke, I felt that at last I had found a form of spirituality that integrated politics and religion in an authentic manner. When we sang, "I Ain't Gonna Let Nobody Turn me Round" or "I Love Everybody," the nonviolent struggle took on both a militancy and a gentleness that I had never experienced before. When the women's choir belted out "Satan, We're Gonna Tear Your Kingdom Down," some deep fearful part of me began to shrink and actually believe that this people's movement could win freedom.

Here was a melding of passion, spirit—even mysticism—and real political struggle that I had been seeking all my life. It was a form of spirituality that led one out on to the street, in particular on to those dusty streets of that once sleepy little Alabama town called Selma.

Thus it came as no surprise that this religious tradition at its best became the source of inspiration and even the home of the Black liberation struggle and that its clergy would often play a leadership role in this revolution. For underneath the issue of voting rights lay the deeper questions of Black rebellion and the uprooting of all those structures and systems which perpetrated oppression in the variety of its economic, social and cultural forms.

After a few days of initiation and indoctrination into this new world of the freedom struggles, the campaign organizers decided that it was time for some of the religious types—often from up North—to join the actual march to Montgomery. A small group of the younger activists had already gone ahead to begin the long march to the Alabama State Capitol and to face the insults and abuse and threats of violence from the crowds along the road that the rest of us would soon be exposed to. This was the third attempt within two weeks by this hardy movement to cross the Pettus Bridge. It was March 21st, the feast of St.

Benedict, our monastic founder, that Aloysius and I set out on this pilgrimage for justice.

National and international press and television exposure as well as the fear of major confrontation and civil unrest had persuaded President Lyndon Johnson to nationalize the Alabama State Guard. The troops lined the road, especially as we marched through more populated areas. None of this seemed to discourage the presence and vociferousness of the white crowds who hurled racist invectives and hateful threats against the marchers. I had feelings of fear that reminded me of my childhood in Germany. Somehow I did not have great confidence in the soldiers' ability (or even sincere desire) to protect us against the members of the Klan and the White Citizens' Council. The armed troops lining the highway appeared steely faced and non-committal, although their very presence created a physical barrier between the marchers and the jeering crowd.

We walked and marched from early in the morning to dusk—seven hot and dusty miles on the first day—with short stops for food and sometimes for common prayer. The marchers knelt on the hard pavement of Highway 80 (also known as the Jefferson Davis Highway) to pray for strength and perseverance and to intercede in a special way for Alabama Governor George Wallace, Sheriff Bill Connor and the sometimes rabidly jeering crowds lining the route of the march. Father Aloysius, more hopefully than I, believed that "our kneeling and praying on that hard concrete and all of us coming together in a peaceful manner must have had an effect even on the police."

It was during one of these rest stops where, as we knelt on the dusty highway for prayer and then nourished ourselves with bologna sandwiches, we were introduced to Dr. Martin Luther King, Jr. My recollection is of a surprisingly short and modest man dressed in a business suit and fedora—who had apparently joined the march freshly returned from the airport and a national speaking engagement. His presence was strong and clear and his brown eyes focused and gentle. He warmly greeted and thanked these two young priests who had traveled from the

North in response to his call for religious people to come and join the struggle. Tears rolled down my cheeks as I sensed the enormity of the moment

It was only a brief handshake and I don't even remember the words, but it was one of the encounters that would change my life. Along with Mahatma Gandhi's teaching on nonviolence, Martin King's vision and teachings would shape my own involvement and commitment for years to come. It would take many of those years for me to realize how far I still was from the deep inner spiritual and psychological conversion that authentic *Satyagraha* (literally clinging to the truth) demanded.

This was the radical doctrine that this slight and modest African-American minister would use to confront the domestic Pax Romana of the most heavily armed empire in human history. Ironically, his principal teacher in this was a small, gaunt Hindu halfway around the world who had reminded him and all of the Christian West of that central (but well hidden) teaching of yet another gaunt, brown-skinned prophet, named Jesus in his Sermon on the Mount.

When Dr. King was unexpectedly cast on the scene of a bus strike in Birmingham, Alabama that would prove to be the spark that ignited the civil rights revolution, he did not arrive with the blueprint of a nonviolent campaign in his back pocket.

This theory and methodology, which embodied the invincible power of transcendent love, even of one's enemies, would later be criticized, attacked and forgotten in the controversies involving the younger Black activists of SNCC (Student Nonviolent Coordinating Committee), the Black Power Movement, the Black Panthers, and especially the charismatic, and later to be martyred, Malcolm X.

It is instructive that the established powers developed a certain strategy of tolerance for Dr. King and his nonviolent movement as long as it limited itself to the issues of voting rights and segregated public accommodations in the South. However, on April 4, 1967 (exactly one year before his assassination), he spoke out against the Vietnam War at the historic Riverside Church in New York City. He stepped out beyond the limits of political propriety in criticizing his own government in a time of war. Even some of his close associates counseled him to refrain from this step into the uncharted waters of war and peace. Yet he was steadfast in this decision to expand the spirit of Satyagraha to the bloody Indochina conflict. He declared, "Some of us who have already begun to break the silence of the night have found that the calling to speak is often a vocation of agony, but we must speak."

But it was his leadership of the Poor Peoples' Campaign that began bringing poor African-Americans, Latinos and Native Americans and whites together in the quest for economic justice, which would symbolize his radical vision of the beloved community and seal his death sentence. Let all those who have sanitized the life and teaching of Martin King, even by the respectability of a national holiday in his honor, take another look at the life and teaching of this Black martyr and great American leader.

Let them go back to the essential writings and speeches of Dr. King (especially those of his later life) to be reminded of how profound, even radical, was his critique of the political and economic system of this nation and how prophetic was his application of nonviolent struggle to the crisis of our times.

One of the best-kept secrets of American history continues to be the truth behind Martin Luther King's execution. At the trial held in Memphis on Nov. 15, 1999 (which was virtually ignored by the media) during the civil suit initiated by the King family, it was determined that the assassination was not the act of an individual racist assassin but a conspiracy of the U.S. government, so hated and feared were the teachings and leadership of this apostle of nonviolence. James Earl Ray eventually denied any role in the murderous plot conceived at a meeting in the office of J. Edgar Hoover and carried out by a sharpshooter of U.S. military intelligence. [1]

---

[1] *An Act of State* by William F. Pepper (the King family's attorney at the trial), Verso 2003.

Dr. King's vision increasingly inflamed my heart and fired my imagination as we marched along that hot and dusty highway on the way to Montgomery and the Alabama State House. Little did I know how profoundly that experience would transform my understanding of Christianity, politics and of life itself.

As we entered the outskirts of the Alabama capital city, the ranks of the marchers began to swell. Hundreds and then thousands from all over the nation joined this sea of humanity as it poured into the metropolis to challenge the century-old foundation of slavery and racial segregation.

Tears ran down my face as we sang the old hymns of a once-slave church, as we became the new Israel calling on the Pharaoh to "Let my people go!" We felt the Spirit come over us as this presumptuous band of "Black and white together" entered the Capitol precincts of one of the most segregated states of America. We were already breathing in the unfamiliar fragrance of the sweet winds of freedom. By this time we had been joined by some significant, more respectable, religious, civic, labor and even a few political leaders and the march had grown from 3,200 to close to 30,000. For me, that day represented a fulfillment of the dream that perhaps justice could triumph after all and that the oppressed people of the earth, even the most despised, might have their day in the sun.

We heard Martin Luther King, Jr., deliver one of his most eloquent speeches from the steps of the Alabama State House itself. It was as if some huge millstone was lifted from my shoulders as I joined with the children and grandchildren of African slaves in this great triumphant procession. The humiliation and fear which I had carried with me all my life from my childhood days in Nazi Germany no longer seemed so powerful and compelling. My tears were tears of joy and celebration. I felt a little embarrassed at the eruption of such deep emotions. There were many eloquent speeches and moving prayers and songs. But it was the message of Dr. King that illuminated the day. Somehow he represented the pride of our movement, the symbol of his people's long and bloody pilgrimage to the light. Even the Confederate flag flying above the state capitol seemed pathetic that day in the face of so much courage and dignity.

As the afternoon sun began to set over the crowd, we slowly and somewhat reluctantly began our return journeys back home. Our joy would not be unalloyed for the next days would bring us news of more bloodshed in the name of violent attempts to maintain the racist status quo. The tragic news came that Viola Liuzzo, the white Unitarian from Detroit whom I had gotten to know, had been murdered as she drove a young Black man to the airport. Now she was gone, another corpse in a Southern morgue to remind us of the long, bitter path that still lay ahead. (With all the appropriate mourning for the killings of Viola Liuzzo and Rev. Reeb, I couldn't help noticing how little public attention had been given to the brutal police shooting in broad daylight two weeks earlier of Jimmie Lee Jackson, a young Black man who had died protecting his mother.)

Father Aloysius and I had befriended an African-American Baptist Church delegation from Philadelphia and they invited us to join their chartered flight back up North. We gladly accepted, eager to maintain the spirit of community and the protection it afforded as we reentered the Southern society at large. We drove to the airport without any great event. However, when our chartered Delta flight landed in Atlanta for refueling, the ground crew there refused to service our plane by emptying the waste from the lavatories or providing any food or refreshment. Thus we were reminded that racism was alive and well and that our work for a just society had only begun.

We returned to our monastery filled with pride and elation, so we were not prepared for a reception that was mixed and tentative at best. The younger monks received us with unabashed enthusiasm and pride that two of their brothers had represented them in this historic campaign for freedom. At the same time, I could sense the unease among the more conservative brethren who feared that this experience would somehow give us—especially me—license to further disrupt the monastic tranquility and isolation with the noise and unrest of "the world."

Their trepidations proved well founded. For from that moment forth my sense of history and of my own vocation as a priest and monk changed profoundly. My inner life of prayer and contemplation was now inhabited by the faces and lives of those I had left behind in Alabama: the Simpson family that housed us, the beautiful school children, the many courageous young freedom fighters, and the suffering Black communities haunted my thoughts and dreams. All too often the hate-filled faces of the people on the road, the members of the Klan and the White Citizens Council would appear before me as well. In meditation in my monastic cell and in our chanting of the Office, these lives of pain and courage began to represent the leitmotif of my spiritual journey. The suffering of the human family, which we as monks presented before the merciful throne of God for healing and protection each day, now took on the particular qualities and aspirations of this crucified community with all of its fears and hopes.

It seemed that the Spirit had brought me to Selma to become not less but more fully a monk. It became clear to me that it was my duty as a Christian priest and monk to cry out against this obscenity in its northern manifestations. Whenever possible I would include the Selma experience and the escalating Vietnam War as examples of the moral implications of the Gospel in retreat lectures and programs. All of this did not sit well with some members of my monastic community.

On one of my Sunday morning parish assignments to celebrate Mass at St. Andrew's parish in Clifton, New Jersey, I mentioned racial justice (and perhaps even the war in Vietnam) in my sermon. Word was sent back to the Abbot that I was not welcome to return as a Sunday morning celebrant.

Thus did I begin my activist career with the direct experience that "Prophets are not without honor, except in their own country and in their own house" (Mt.13:57). It would not be the last time that I would experience this pain of being attacked or at least not supported by my own community and church at large. It would be an even longer process—one that is still going on—before I would realize the challenge of forgiving "the enemy within" and seek reconciliation if not agreement with those who were my own.

The words of Dr. Martin Luther King, Jr., in his historic address on March 21, 1965 at the Montgomery State House at the end of the Selma march continued to be a challenge to my spiritual and political journey.

The musical cadences of his words will continue to sound within me like a great bell, acting as a powerful antidote to the hopelessness that often lurks at the perimeter of my consciousness. These almost magical sounds still have the power to contradict and heal the despair threatening to invade my soul as I feel overwhelmed by the world's pain and injustice and my own sense of powerlessness:

> "Our aim must never be to defeat or humiliate the white man but to win his friendship and understanding. We must come to see that the end we seek is a society at peace with itself, a society that can live with its conscience. That will be a day not of the white man, not of the Black man. That will be the day of man as man.

> "I know you are asking today, "How long will it take?" I come to say to you this afternoon however difficult this moment, however frustrating the hour, it will not be long, because truth pressed to earth will rise again.

> "How long? Not long, because no lie can live forever.

> "How long? Not long, because you will reap what you sow.

> "How long? Not long. Because the arc of the moral universe is long but it bends toward justice.

> "How long? Not long, 'cause mine eyes have seen the glory of the coming of the Lord, trampling out the vintage where the grapes of wrath are stored. He has loosed the fateful lightning of His terrible swift sword. His truth is marching on.

"He has sounded forth the trumpets that shall never call retreat. He is lifting up the hearts of man before His judgment seat. Oh, be swift, my soul, to answer Him. Be jubilant, my feet. Our God is marching on."

Paul Mayer's more than half century of service to the earth included eighteen years as a Benedictine monk, involvement in the civil rights movement in the South, work in the barrios of Central America, participation in the effort to end the war in Vietnam as well as co-founding peace and environmental organizations.

Mayer's childhood experience as a Jewish refugee from Nazi Germany inspired him to co-found Children of War, a youth leadership organization that helped transform the lives of teenage survivors of international and domestic wars. While still a monk, he spent time in Panama applying the tenets of liberation theology to parish and community work. He worked with Jesse Jackson in the Rainbow Coalition and addressed the Democratic Convention in 1984 on nuclear disarmament.

Mayer served as coordinator of the Catonsville Nine Defense Committee in support of religious non-violent actions during the Vietnam War by the Fathers Daniel and Philip Berrigan and others. In 1978 he founded the Religious Task Force, a national network to convene the various faith communities to work together on issues of peace and social justice.

His peace and justice ministry has taken him to Japan to work with atom bomb survivors. He traveled to Cuba with Pastors for Peace to challenge the U.S. blockade by bringing humanitarian aid to the churches and to the Middle East for reconciliation work in the conflict between Israelis and Palestinians.

He was a founder of the New Jersey Sea Alliance calling for the joint abolition of nuclear weapons and power after the Harrisburg nuclear accident. In the 1970s he was the founder of a spiritual peace community in inner-city East Orange, NJ.

His work for peace and with indigenous people has taken him to the United Nations Earth Summit in Rio de Janeiro in 1992 and to

Johannesburg, South Africa in 2002. Paul was involved with United for Peace and Justice and the New York City Forum of Concerned Religious Leaders in work for peace and justice in Iraq and the Gulf region. In 2009 he spoke at one of the events of the UN Climate Change Conference in Copenhagen.

Mayer was cofounder of the Climate Crisis Coalition, started in 2003 to convey a sense of urgency around the climate crisis and to broaden the constituency of this overarching issue beyond the traditional environmental organizations. He also helped form the Interfaith Moral Action on Climate Change (IMAC) in 2012.

Mayer's commitment to global peace, social justice, ecology, non-violent social change explores the link between spirituality and activism. He had an active wedding ministry as a non-canonical, formerly married priest.

In 2010 he was awarded the Komacki Fellowship of the Virginia Center for the Creative Arts for nonfiction writing which "celebrates the behind-the-scenes story of an activist striving to make his or her vision of a more perfect world a reality" for *Wrestling With Angels: A Spiritual Memoir of a Political Life*.

He remained a priest and had an active wedding ministry. In 2013 Mayer was diagnosed with brain cancer. He died November 22 that year at his home in East Orange, N.J. (The above essay is taken from Chapter 6 of *Wrestling With Angels*.)

Michael Kiesow Moore

The End of War

It is not an easy path to believe in peace. The moment you say out loud words like "nonviolence" or "pacifism," it is as if you threw down a gauntlet. Fighting words. People suddenly have so much to say about how wrong such ideas are, naïve, that violent action must be taken to end conflict, and so on. It gets tiring, hearing all the reasons I should step off my path and think like everyone else.

In some respects I have always believed in peace. Always felt a rightness to the way of nonviolence. As a child I was drawn deeply to the stories of Martin Luther King, Jr. and Mahatma Gandhi, my first superheroes. And then something happened to me when I was 12 years old. What happened on this one day, and the vow I made in its aftermath, solidified my commitment to peace. Decades after what happened I am still haunted by that event, and find myself continuously shaped and reshaped by a quiet vow my 12-year-old self-made in the face of overwhelming despair.

The bullies I faced in elementary school were like the heads of the Hydra; just as one disappeared and I thought I was finally safe, two appeared to take its place. It really did not matter who they were. Instead of mean boys who taunted and beat me up, it was more like a malevolent spirit that continued haunting me. No matter the shape, it remained the same. Hatred embodied. The first words thrown at me were "fatso," "sissy," and "cry baby." After a while they dropped "cry baby" because I taught myself to keep from crying, learning how to bottle up my feelings inside. You acquire such tactics in order to survive.

When I moved on to middle school, I hoped—prayed—that the bullying would stop, that I would finally escape my tormentors.

I did not escape. It got worse, as did the types of names I was called. The bullying escalated, worsening year after year. I eventually became a truant in high school to escape the bullies. In college someone painted "faggot" on my dormitory door, and someone threatened to kill me. But the story I want tell, the story of an event that solidified my commitment to nonviolence, takes place in middle school.

By seventh grade, the malevolent spirit that haunted me took the form of a boy named Randy, who one day challenged me to a fight. I did not know why he wanted to fight me. I was fat. He wasn't. I was a sissy. He had to prove that he was not. I was gay, although at 12 years old I did not have the words yet to articulate this to even myself. Perhaps Randy was gay, too, and that was why he had to fight me. In me he may have seen a reflection that he could not live with; by destroying it, he sought to destroy that part of him he hated. Surprisingly, that day he challenged me, I said yes. The adage I learned in Sunday school, to turn my cheek to my enemies, only led to more name calling and getting beat up. I did teach myself to stop crying from those taunts, but ending having feelings did not go so well. The names hurt. I decided not to take it anymore.

Word spread throughout the school. The time was set 2:00 p.m., in the boys' bathroom. At the appointed hour I headed towards the place of combat. As I slowly walked there, I changed my mind. I did not want to go through with it, even though I would lose face. Given a choice between honor with a broken nose, or disgrace with an intact body, I decided that I did not want the blood. What had I been thinking?

A mob of boys and girls had now formed and they pushed me toward the bathroom. I could not escape, even though I struggled to. I fought to get away, but they pulled me into the boys' bathroom. Everything went into fast motion as I got to the door. Next thing I knew, the mob shoved me into the bathroom where Randy waited for me.

Once thrust into that bathroom, Randy commenced an onslaught of blows at my head. All I could do was try to deflect them while a thick mass of boys and girls behind me prevented escape. A teacher's voice soon sounded. The jubilant cries of "fight, fight!" and "get him" subsided. Finally the blows ceased. The students were made to return to their classes and Randy and I were taken to separate places for interrogation.

One of my favorite teachers, Miss Diemer—the reading teacher, my favorite subject—led my cross-examination. What she asked over and over was, why didn't I have a pass to go to the bathroom? Prior to this incident, the teachers had made a big to-do that you had to have a pass to go to the bathroom, perhaps to forestall incidents like this, or other sorts of misbehaviors. She did not ask me why a swarm of boys and girls had descended on me. She did not ask if there was anything she could do to help me. She did not even ask if I was okay. Nobody, not her, not anyone, ever asked if I was hurt. What her insistent question told me—one I gave no answer to because it was the wrong question—was that I had no allies. Not adults, especially teachers. I did not tell my parents what happened that day, nor about any of the other of the worst days of violence because I was too embarrassed. For all they knew, I liked school and perhaps thought I was safe. The shame of what I lived with day after day froze my voice.

That young boy I once was stood solitary in a world that did not want to understand me.

As I lay in bed that night after the fight, I realized that what had me the most chagrined about that sad fight was my own betrayal of my ethics. Nothing could justify it, not even my desperation to be like everyone else. I was made to turn into somebody who could say yes to fighting. That night, while I nursed my bruises, real and emotional, I made a vow: no fighting, ever.

I look back at my 12-year-old self and I feel proud of him. Knowing that there was no end in sight of the bullying and no one would ever have his back—in the face of all that—still he said to himself: never again. Fighting was not the answer. It never was and never would be. It took strength to believe that. I would even say courage.

I now look back at that time with feelings of outrage. Why did this boy have to face all this violence alone? He could not tell his parents what happened out of the shame he felt. But his teachers saw what was being done to him. Only once did a teacher say something to me about being bullied. It was in elementary school, and after a brutal beating on the playground my fifth-grade teacher walked me to the nurse's office and said, "Why don't you learn to fight back?" At the age of ten years old I learned that adults were going to be useless.

I hope that today there is better understanding of bullying and there are more compassionate teachers in schools than the ones I endured. Teachers who saw the violence done to me and did less than nothing are perhaps the worst villains in my story.

I recently wrote a poem titled, "The Bully." In the course of the poem I summarize all the brutality, concluding, "The fear of you haunted my every day." And then I note a kind of triumph. ". . . I have captured you here in this poem". But I do not gloat. The poem concludes,

> I will feed you words to sustain you.
> I will offer you space to grow.
> I will hope you find love.
> I will pray for your transformation.
> I will offer many prayers.

Many have asked about how I was able to take such a journey to forgiveness. In the end, what else can you do? Hold anger in your heart the rest of your life? I was not able to do it then, but today I can begin to see these bullies as human beings. Perhaps they were abused themselves. One of the bullies who was the neighborhood scourge shot his father. What kind of violence did he suffer behind closed doors to take such an action?

I feel less forgiving toward the teachers who saw my torments. I am still angry at them. Perhaps I have further to go in my journey of forgiveness. The fact is that young people are killing themselves in droves right now. In the suburbs of the Twin Cities young people were killing themselves so often that the story made the cover of *Rolling Stone* and lawsuits led to anti-bullying efforts that many in that community continue to fight against. While writing this essay there have been further suicides of youth, especially by young transgender people.

Why does it have to be so hard for anyone who does not fit into culturally circumscribed squares and round holes? Shouldn't there be a place in our world for sensitive souls, for young people who feel that Male or Female do not fit, for anyone whose sexual preference is not exactly for the opposite sex? Can we not have a place in schools and communities for the dreamers and peace keepers?

Children know who they are. It is up to the adults to make it possible for them to grow up to meet their full potential. The adults who turn blind eyes to the violence done against the children in their care are equally responsible for that violence.

It is not easy looking back at this time. Nor is it easy telling this story. When you grow up with a voice frozen by shame, decades later it is still hard to speak of these times. My hands shake as I type these words.

I still see so clearly the tender-hearted child I once was lying in bed after that fight in school, silently crying, feeling helpless and so utterly alone. Nevertheless, in the face of that terrible anguish, he said to himself "For now on, only nonviolence." The end of war, the end of violence, begins with me.

May I do justice to that boy's long-held vow.

Michael Kiesow Moore is an award-winning writer of fiction, creative nonfiction, and poetry, and author of the poetry collection *What to Pray For* (Nodin Press). Among many awards, he has received a Minnesota State Arts Board fellowship and a Loft Mentor Series Award, and received nominations for the Pushcart Prize for poetry and the Minnesota Book Award. He has published short stories, poetry, and essays in journals and magazines including *The Saint Paul Almanac, Talking Stick, Rockhurst Review, Water~Stone Review, Evergreen Chronicles, Peacework, The James White Review, Mpls. St. Paul Magazine*, and in the book, *A Loving Testimony: Losing Loved Ones Lost to AIDS*. Most recently, he has poetry anthologized in *Among the Leaves: Queer Male Poets on the Midwestern Experience*.

Moore was born in Cheyenne, Wyoming and grew up in Florida and Maryland. A transplant to Minnesota, he enjoys the thriving writing and artistic community there. He received a B.A. magna cum laude from Towson University with special honors and a MFA. in Creative Writing at Hamline University, receiving the Outstanding Thesis award. Moore is the founder and co-curator for the Birchbark Books Reading Series at Birchbark Books in Minneapolis, an independent bookstore.

Moore teaches creative writing and is an instructor at the Loft Literary Center.

Jacqueline Mosio

Scenes from a Life

What is a life? What are our lives? We yearned for a new world, keenly sensing that there were other ways to be as individuals and as a society. We banded together, struggled, lived, learned, lost, and scattered. We stood, facing the horizon, straining to see what was to be revealed.

Scene: Prague. August 20-21, 1969. The anniversary of the Russian invasion that brought an end to the Prague Spring. I was there on purpose. I had followed these events: the hopefulness of liberalization in Czechoslovakia under reformist Alexander Dubček, the crushing finality of the 200,000 invading Eastern Bloc troops and their 2,000 tanks, and the resistance of the Czech people. Jan Palach, a 20-year-old history and political economy student, had set himself ablaze in protest in Wenceslas Square in January.

Wenceslas Square is the town center of Prague where streets and the old tram lines crossed the several-block rectangle. At noon on August 20th everything stopped. Silence filled the Square and surrounding streets. The old buildings almost looked startled at the sudden silence. It was the only protest that could be risked. That evening I was in the Square with newfound friends—a Romanian student, a German doctor, a young Irish traveler. Wenceslas Square was full of commuters changing trams and making their way home when the occupying army moved in and announced via bullhorns that the Square must be cleared immediately. We began running to escape the soldiers and their batons. The jostling crowd squeezed into the narrow streets beyond the Square. Our path took us in front of the Czech National Museum where earlier someone had pointed out the bullet pockmarks left from the invasion a year ago. We were moving as fast as we could. Behind me was a soldier, his arm raised. The baton thwacked my shoulders. In that instant I viscerally understood power and its misuse. The impact of that blow went beyond the Russians, the Czech people and their lost hope. Clearing the Square was a contrived operation to terrorize and abuse the population, to remind them who was in control. And this is the same pattern of all oppressive, overreaching and power-hungry states. That insight informed my stance in the face of all official repression.

Scene: A convent situated above the mighty Mississippi River. I am one of nearly sixty young women who are considering becoming members of a teaching order of Catholic nuns. We have been discussing poverty as part of Catholic social teaching. I wonder how I can express solidarity with the poor in a situation where I am fed and taken care of. I have a place to sleep even though it is a simple bed in a dormitory of ten and my space is partitioned by cloth curtains that we tie back with a clatter of metal rings against metal rods as we leave for early morning prayer and Mass.

Ah, I know what I'll do. I will sleep without blankets like poor people are forced to do. Homelessness wasn't as prevalent then as it is now, but I knew the poor throughout the world suffered from not having adequate sleeping conditions.

The first night of my experiment I shivered throughout the night. My blankets remained folded at the foot of my bed. The cold didn't let me sleep. The next day I pushed myself through our tasks and classes. The next night the same. I would fall asleep briefly but wake up thoroughly chilled and only able to sleep fitfully. By the third day of my experiment I was unable to function. I was falling asleep during religious instructions. I could barely complete my cleaning tasks and moved as if drugged. I didn't enjoy my companions at recreation hour. I felt remote and disconnected. I only wanted to sleep but couldn't break from our schedule to nap. So this is what happens when you can't sleep because you are cold—or hungry or frightened because of violence. I never forgot that experience.

Is there a social justice gene? If there is, that might explain why I earnestly watched news programs and tried to come up with solutions to the grave problems I heard about—the Cold War, food shortages—at age six. I would drop off to sleep pondering the news and ways to solve the world's problems. Is this an instinct we have? If so, it's underdeveloped, underutilized and undervalued.

Scene I: On the lawn of the Smithsonian Institute. I was fourteen and on a trip to Washington DC with a friend and her family. A middle-aged woman speaking with what to me was a Southern drawl stood at a table covered with racist literature. She spewed comments about how Blacks and whites should be separate, how unfit and inferior Blacks were as a race, and so forth. I had never heard such comments "live" although I had read them and been in discussions about prejudice. I studied her and others in her audience awhile and then approached her table. She thought she had a convert and handed me a pamphlet.

I figured she probably considered herself a "good Christian woman" so I asked her "Are you planning on going to heaven when you die?" She answered in the affirmative. "Well then," I continued, "what will you do when you meet Blacks there?" She opened her mouth to say something but instead turned away from me. I couldn't tell if she was flummoxed or just disdainful of this brash northern kid, but she remained silent behind her table piled with hate-filled literature.

It was no small irony that my time working in Washington DC after college was replete with racial incidents.

Scene II: I was teaching English in a suburban Maryland school but lived near the DC border by New Hampshire Avenue. Arriving home from school I looked down New Hampshire toward DC. The avenue was filled with army tanks. In the distance smoke rose over the capital. This was April 4, 1968. Martin Luther King, Jr. had just been assassinated. DC was burning.

Scene III: The Cherry Blossom Festival. One of the festival's events was held on a stage in a park and open to the public. Many African-American families came with their children to watch the presentation of the Cherry Blossom Princesses chosen by members of each state society in DC. Young officers from branches of the military served as escorts for the princesses. I had been chosen to represent Minnesota. I mockingly called myself the "Cherry Pit Princess" but enjoyed participating in the festivities which included a visit to the White House, a meeting with the Japanese ambassador, a tree planting ceremony with Joan Kennedy, various lunches, a parade, and a formal ball.

On this particular sunny April afternoon, the program called for each escort to stand in front of the curtain and announce the name of the princess and her state. Then she would step through the curtain and be escorted across the stage. About halfway through the program, the escort for Michigan said at the microphone, "Before I present the next princess to you, I would like to mention and apologize for the fact that there are no princesses that reflect the diversity of the United States and its territories."

Behind the curtain there were gasps and moans. "This is what causes riots," one chaperone cried. But the show went on. The princess from Michigan was unfazed and had probably planned this with her escort.

From that moment, though, the entire group—princesses and escorts—polarized. Those who agreed with the officer's statement found each other and, in the short time we had, participated in the spontaneous protests and gatherings that were continually going on in DC at the time. The *Washington Post* gave an odd and inaccurate account of the incident so I wrote a letter to the paper that was published. My venture into Princess politics.

Scene I: The lawn of the U.S. embassy in Paris, November 1969. A group of Americans living in Paris has organized to protest the war in Vietnam. Dozens of white wooden crosses are planted in the small space of green. A member of the Paris American Friends Service Committee, a Quaker working with Thich Nhat Hanh, takes us to meet him. We begin a three-day protest fast. There are maybe forty of us.

Scene II: Thanksgiving Dinner for American students studying in Paris. Our group of fasters files in and stands silently along the walls around the dining hall as the names of the war dead are slowly read. A woman in our group, weak from fasting, sinks to the floor. Most of the students ignore us, but some stand with us briefly before the protest action ends.

At the start of sixth grade, I pulled a textbook from a shelf in my classroom. It was about Minnesota history including the Dakota and Chippewa. I asked the teacher when we were going to study this book. Later in the year, she said and told me to put the book back. We never opened those books.

We are always missing, ignoring, overlooking, blocking out and covering up our real history. This is living in denial. We can no longer do this and survive as a society.

Scene I: Cuernavaca, Mexico. January 1970. Besides being a good place to be in winter, Ivan Illich's Centro Internacional de Documentación (CIDOC) was intellectually alive and accessible far beyond any university setting. Illich, a former monsignor in the Catholic Church, was proposing new forums for education, buffeting the Western medical system, attacking status quo economics, and trying to de-program Christian missionaries heading to South America. His success and notoriety attracted hundreds of curious participants to his venture in the hills overlooking Cuernavaca. The message of his books *Deschooling Society* and *Medical Nemesis* rumbled through academia and roiled intellectuals around the world.

Young Mexicans taught Spanish to those who came to study at CIDOC while intellectuals, academics, and anyone Illich wanted to engage with offered conferences and workshops in the intense atmosphere. It was also an unparalleled opportunity to learn about Latin America. I met a refugee lawyer from Brazil, liberation theology priests, an American whose Guatemalan friend had been captured by the army and pushed out of a helicopter. Eric Fromm, Paulo Freire, Paul Goodman, and Jonathan Kozol were some of the featured visitors.

Just outside the house in the coffee shop patio, Celerina, an indigenous woman from a Nahuatl-speaking village in the state of Guerrero, sold brightly painted *amates* or bark paintings that featured stylized birds, flowers, animals and village scenes. Celerina's husband had gone to the States as part of a bracero program and when he failed to return, her children and property were divided up among her relatives and she was left to fend for herself and her youngest daughter. I arranged for her to give a presentation in the CIDOC garden and provided English interpretation as she told her story of how she became a successful Mexican craft vendor. In all her years selling there, she had never been inside the large house.

The first Earth Day was celebrated April 22 that year and I organized the commemoration at CIDOC. The people Illich attracted and the intellectual foment generated during the CIDOC years continue to have impact.

Scene II: A gathering of friends. September 1973. We are in shock about the coup d'état that deposed Chilean President

Salvador Allende on September 11. Someone comes with the news that Charles Horman, an American journalist and writer who visited Cuernavaca with his wife Joyce on their way to Santiago de Chile, is missing and presumed dead. We knew them. Charles' father would later travel to Chile to try to find his son's body and piece together what happened to him and who was responsible for his death. The Costa-Gavras movie *Missing* tells that story of the father's search and the U.S. involvement in the coup.

Within a few months hundreds of Chileans begin arriving in Mexico, released from prisons and torture houses.

Scene III: The small garden outside my house. It is dark and I am holding a two-year-old boy in my arms. He reaches for the reflection of the full moon in the birdbath. His mother is hospitalized in Mexico City. Her friends are taking care of her child. They were all arrested, beaten and tortured, they tell me, but her injuries are so serious that she will not survive.

I learned from my travels that if things could be a little different in society, they could be a lot different, radically different. Poverty and discrimination are not absolutes but products of history and economic forces. Why can't society support its members instead of so often crushing them?

Scene: A discussion club meeting. Berkeley 1971. A middle-aged woman with water-blue eyes sits listening to others speak. She wears a green sweatshirt with darkish brown stain marks. No one says anything because the woman is blind, and her friends figure she didn't realize she put on soiled clothing. Finally, she speaks up. "I'm sure you all noticed my sweatshirt but are too polite to say anything. I lent this sweatshirt to my young friend Jackie who went to the beach to help rescue the birds soaked by the oil from the spill. She told me how she held the ducks and tried to wipe off the gummy oil. Most of them will die. But we will still have gas for our cars."

Scene: A national forest in southern Oregon. I am high up in a tall, thick-trunked pine tree. The task at hand is collecting pinecones for the commune's pine tree farm. Fragrant, gummy pine resin sticks to my hands and clothes. The resin collects stray pine needles. The climber's rope firmly clasps me to the trunk. I reach for, snatch and cache pine cones in a sack slung over my shoulder. I stop and listen to the wind as it softly sifts through the branches. I feel the tree's swaying response. This is pine tree life and I am privileged to know it so intimately. There's something like love and humbleness in the encounter.

Later, as I remove the copious resin from my hands and clothes, I realize with satisfaction that the whisper of pine wind will remain with me forever.

For me there was no one moment that set me on my path. It was more of an ongoing dialogue with reality, with life that deepened my understanding. A growing awareness was fed by others, by experience, reading, learning. Something within responds and recognizes the truth of things.

Scene: Tepotzlán, Mexico. An expansive room in a large house in front of an oversize fireplace with a glowing fire. Women, mostly from the United States, but also a French academic and a Mexican woman, have gathered to talk about our reality and experience as women. The air crackles and seethes as we explore and share our wounds, frustrations, losses, beatings, insults, physical attacks, and struggles in a world that is dominated by a specific male viewpoint that regards us, because we are female, as inferior.

Scene: A hill beyond the industrial port of Lázaro Cárdenas, Michoacán. I'm taking a photo of a woman in front of a flimsy shack where her three very young children are sitting on a mat. Nearly a hundred desperately poor families had built cardboard and corrugated metal shacks along a ridge. Construction, steel factory, and other work in the government's development zone offer a way out of poverty. People from all across Mexico migrated to the west coast in hopes of finding work.

I was teaching photography at the local Casa de la Cultura cultural center and worked with my students to document the dramatic changes in the region. In this case I was photographing the damage caused by a flood that had washed away houses in the settlement and filled others with mud. The woman in the shack casually mentions that the smallest baby will be dead in a day.

Scene: La Casa de la Cultura, Lázaro Cárdenas, Michoacán. An evening class. My American friend Ann Roy presents her slideshow "What the Devil Happened to the Goddess?" to a group of women from the community. An art historian and artist, she researched and compiled images of women from the earliest lumps of clay honoring fertility through the smiling and benevolent goddesses produced in many cultures. But at some point, the images change dramatically, and the feminine is represented by the terrifying Medusa head and the fierce Mexican Coatlicue with her skirt of writhing serpents and necklace of hearts and severed hands. It gets worse. Contemporary images show the goddess and the feminine reduced to a sex symbol used to sell cars and other products or an object of derision—a woman with six breasts and one with a viperous snake for a tongue. Ann poses the question: Do these images represent fear and rejection of the feminine and signal a major shift or disconnect in consciousness that results in deep fissures in human society?

The discussion unleashes bursts of energy and realization of the great feminine power that all the women know they are connected to. They are joyful and enthusiastic about this new vision and ask for a continuation of the class the following day.

The next morning Ann and I arrive at the Casa de la Cultura eager to hear the women share their stories and insights. We wait. No one comes. Finally, one woman shows up, but she's only dropping her child off for a class. She says that she told her husband about the slideshow and discussion and he forbade her to come back.

Does it all come down to consciousness? To an awareness of our truth? What is it that is so feared and denies the humanity of others?

Scene: My living room. 11 PM. Phone rings. "Jackie, is this a good time to talk?" It's midnight in New Jersey, and Paul Mayer is calling for our editing session. He was, I'm sure, often annoyed at my suggestions, cuts, and requests for rewrites, but he was unfailingly kind to his "editorturer" as I called myself. Paul was also an engaging, eloquent writer with a keen sense of humor, which meant our late-night conferences were punctuated with much laughter. Paul was in his late seventies when I began working with him on *Wrestling with Angels: A Spiritual Memoir of a Political Life.*

As I learned more about this activist priest, a Holocaust refugee and convert from Judaism, and his over fifty years of political action, I reviewed my own life and checked my levels of political fervor and commitment. That was a humbling experience. Paul, with his outstanding talent for political action and organization, founded groups, formed committees, planned marches, events, and protests. He confronted the FBI and the police, and was arrested often. He traveled on international peace-making missions, addressed world gatherings and national conventions, and led prayers for justice. He struggled daily to live out his beliefs and ideals. His memoir is not just his—it's the memoir of an age, a review of recent history recounted by one who was lived it.

We worked together for several years via phone before I met Paul in New York. I encountered a man of slight build with clear blue eyes and white hair. He radiated a peaceful intensity and a sense of steady focus. He taught yoga, but I sensed that the deep aura around him also came from other sources.

I had a question in my mind as we started our work. Over the years many activists stepped back, retired, even abandoned or at least took breaks from organizing, speaking out, networking, formulating plans and carrying them out. But Paul didn't. In the 1980s, when many of us pulled away, Paul co-founded Children of War that brought together young people from conflict areas around the world for healing and to reach out to peers in the U.S. through speaking tours.

As I edited his compelling memoir, it was obvious that Paul never pulled back, retired or left off being an activist. This led me to another question: How did he do it? I wanted to know what motivated him and kept his hopes and spirit burning bright. I had to know because I did pull away, become disillusioned, disheartened, lost faith, and exempted myself from participation in political activity. I never gave up my beliefs and hopes, but I no longer extended myself or got involved beyond following developments or serving on the board of the Resource Center of the Americas as that organization wound down. I no longer believed I could make a difference.

Paul often told me that he was writing *Wrestling with Angels* to show how one person can make a difference. But how did he keep his faith? Was it his deep spirituality from his years as a monk? Was it revering and heeding the messages of Israel's prophets? Did his experiences with Native American teachers and his love of nature put a special seal on his soul? Paul never articulated an easy answer to my question, but I understood that he never lost faith in his ability to make a difference.

Encountering that firm faith during the years of working with Paul as his "editorturer" nudged me back onto the often painful path of responding to our society's need for peace and justice activists.

What is a life? What impact do our lives have? What's the meaning of this vast tapestry with interweavings, crossed strands, broken threads? I've barely mentioned the Women's Movement and its impact on my life and the solidarity that developed among women. I haven't talked about the part poetry and writing played in my life. Nor communal living, an attempted ideal for several years. Or what being a Spanish medical interpreter for immigrants in the Twin Cities meant to me.

Disillusionment and discouragement sapped my energy. Compared to many others who set their sights on social ills and worked decades to change society, I really did not do much. However, I did conscientiously hone my awareness and understanding of how the economic system operates, who has power and who doesn't and why, and confronted bias toward myself and other women because we were women, and toward people of other races. I observed groups working for justice and their attempts to impact society and tried to figure out what promotes effective change.

A generation of us stood facing the horizon waiting and working for the revelation of a new world.

What was revealed was ourselves.

Jacqueline Mosio My interest now is in working within my local community to increase awareness of environmental, social justice, and diversity issues as a large portion of our area is converted from a former Ford assembly plant to what we hope will be a livable, walkable, accessible, sustainable, diverse neighborhood that serves as a model for development practices. The Highland Community Initiative is a grassroots organization dedicated to building the community that will be the future community. Previous work as a Spanish medical interpreter forged ties to the local immigrant community.

I am currently working with Maria Nhambu as her editor ("editormentor") for her memoir *Africa's Child*, the first book in her Dancing Soul Trilogy, and *America's Daughter*, the second book.

Ray Myers

Changed During the Sixties

Bouncing over and around potholes on a dusty dirt road in a jammed Indian public transit bus, a man asked me if I knew that Kennedy had been assassinated. "Yes, I did," but that happened some years before in November 1963. This was now June 1968, my last month of service in the Peace Corps in Mysore State (now Karnataka). But he was not talking about John Kennedy. This was news about his brother, Bobby, who was now running for the Democratic nomination to be President of the United States. In his hand he was holding the local newspaper written in Kannada, which also included a photo of the fallen Kennedy lying on the kitchen floor of the Ambassador Hotel in Los Angeles. Two months earlier, Martin Luther King was assassinated in Memphis as he walked on his motel's balcony. I heard that news on a BBC broadcast on our short-wave radio a few days after the event. The only printed news confirming his death came later by way of Indian postal delivery of two-week bundles of the Sunday Review section of the *New York Times*.

My days as a Volunteer in northern Karnataka were quickly ending in terms of my service there and I was already thinking about what heroic return I could make to the United States. I had already "saved" a small part of the world and I thought I should start applying those skills to someplace closer to home. Born in Philadelphia with my family now living in southern New Jersey, why not return to the city of my birth and offer my skills to the needy children of that city where a new young superintendent was actively recruiting a fresh cadre of teachers who were more idealistic, more adventuresome, ready for a new challenge on their "home turf" after spending a few years abroad where they had survived and learned to live and adapt to a different culture with a new language and culture half way around the globe. My diet would also change to vegetarian simply because of living and surviving in a predominantly Hindu society where meat consumption was forbidden. What I did not realize was that the city where I wanted to work had also changed dramatically during my years in India. My idealism far exceeded my ability to succeed in an environment that was now more foreign to me than the streets of Dharwad, Karnataka. Although I had taught health and nutrition at a Teacher Training Institute in India, I was not in the least prepared to teach third and fourth grade students in an urban elementary school in September 1968. Nor was I prepared to witness the riots at the Democratic National Convention in August that year.

Even before I left India I had made plans to teach in Philadelphia that coming September. I landed at the Philadelphia International Airport on a hot muggy summer afternoon. This was the summer of the riotous Democratic National Convention in Chicago. The television screens were now full of the nightly battles between police and demonstrators protesting festering social and political injustices of the American system, the foremost being the continuation of the war in Vietnam. These scenes were clearly foreign to the vast majority of American and international viewers. For me, watching television in itself was something that I had not experienced over the past two years. It was a fresh, unnerving look at the power of the media to record and report the disturbing realities of the upheaval in the late 1960s for Americans accustomed to more peaceful views of our political processes. They now saw young Americans who vowed they were not going to fight for American intrusion in a foreign land. Neither were they going to be conscripted to fight these wars at the behest of their political leaders.

The years that I had spent in the Peace Corps in India were idyllic in comparison to the turmoil at home. The war in Vietnam clearly dominated any discussion of U.S. foreign policy. We may have a Peace Corps, but are we really able to make the world, and perhaps more importantly, the United States, a safer and more peaceful place? Even more than the war, Americans now began to see that their true identities were more associated with the color of their skins than the place of their birth. Soul singer James Brown's "Say It Loud, I'm Black and I'm Proud" became a national anthem.

So in a matter of two months from the termination of my Peace Corps service I was to become an elementary school teacher in urban Philadelphia. A neighboring school system near my home town in New Jersey also offered me a position teaching social studies in their high school, a position for which I was better qualified. After interviewing and being offered the position, I declined in favor of pursuing the more idealistic challenge of working in an urban non-white school setting, at an instructional level for which I was totally unprepared. I was oblivious to what I would have to do to prepare for such a new challenge. For me summer months back in southern New Jersey meant that I would have more time to return to the shore where I could once again resume the seasonal cycle of days on the beaches and nights in the bars near the ocean. This was now a time for feasting after two years of famine where alcohol was rationed and couples' dating was strictly prohibited. While some friends had serious romantic relationships, I was unattached and not interested in any serious commitments. Perhaps I felt I had earned some time to simply enjoy myself before making a deeper commitment to a teaching career in the coming months. In the Jersey shore bars, the specter of the Vietnam War was clearly in the air. Young men who had been in Vietnam and escaped its ravages were grateful to be having a summer at home. Others who knew their time was coming through the draft or their current military status were trying to forget what the future might bring. It was all part of the working class culture and responsibility. Hardly anyone in those summer hangouts had a father who had not fought in World War II or other American conflicts. This was seen as a patriotic duty for healthy young Americans. We had stopped Hitler and we felt a responsibility to protect our allies when their freedoms were endangered. We trusted our political leaders to make these decisions when necessary and responded to answer the call to bear arms. In the late sixties with Vietnam and the impact of our returning veterans, Americans were now coming to the realization that our world has many dangers that perhaps could not all be solved by war alone.

After this respite of days on the beaches and nights at the bars, I was about to plunge into the urban challenge that awaited me. The years in India were a world-expanding experience that was a revelation to me. I had studied western European history in college, but I actually got to live in a part of the world where west did meet east. My mind had been opened beyond any amount of history lectures that I could have possibly attended. Surely I could return home to the city of my birth and apply these newly honed skills to the challenges in urban American public education.

All of my students in that 4th/5th grade combination classroom on the ground floor of a three-story brick schoolhouse, in the shadows of the Ben Franklin Bridge, were black. The Principal's office was directly across the hall. He was white and ready to retire. With few exceptions, the teachers were female and black. I was called to his office often, primarily because my classroom was out of control. I was unprepared. Those years teaching in India and student teaching in college had not prepared me to teach in this setting. I was back home, but not in a place I had ever visited or worked in before.

Another culture had been my home for the past 21 months. I had acclimated with relative ease to many of the customs, language, food, and daily routine of living in a small town in India. As a health and nutrition teacher at a Teacher Training Institute in Dharwad, I also oversaw the construction of school kitchens in neighboring villages where the children received CARE's mid-day meal of *uppittu* (made with bulgur wheat) and milk (from powder). The CARE midday meal feeding program provided half the costs of the actual construction. The kitchens were intended to be models for the sanitary and secure storage of the CARE commodities so that they would not spoil or be stolen. Smoke from the wood fires would fill the kitchen area with potential damage to the cooks' vision. The mud stoves in the kitchens were designed to be "smokeless" when constructed properly with a chimney to draw the smoke away. My teaching duties were minimal so I spent most of my workdays involved in travel and meetings with neighboring village leaders, primary school principals and teachers. During my time there, I worked with approximately a dozen village headmasters and leaders in constructing kitchens at their schools.

It was much easier for me than for our female volunteers who were more restricted in their ability to mingle in the predominantly male-oriented world. I looked like a stereotypical young American from a suburban setting which made my acceptance easier, while also inviting more attention and curiosity from strangers. Only men felt comfortable enough to address me directly in the market place or while traveling on public transportation. This directness was also a much different experience than any encounters they may have had with the previous British rulers. We were as foreign to our Indian hosts as they were to us, with little or no understanding on their part as to why we were there. It was a much more defined world during the years of British rule. Class and caste seemed to be accepted as being compatible systems of governing a country. As a young visitor to the Indian world I could very objectively analyze this time of transition from foreign occupation to democratization led by Gandhi, his family and followers. It was much easier to observe as an outsider than to have a "stake" in the political outcome. I came to realize this more personally when I returned home after my Peace Corps service.

Social and political change was happening at home and I was soon to realize its impact on my own plans and aspirations. Philadelphia Public Schools would give returned Peace Corps volunteers an opportunity to apply their idealism in an urban setting where they could conceivably use skills they may have learned abroad. But I was more a foreigner in an American urban school system in 1968 than I had been the previous two years in India. I knew less about African-American life in this city than I knew about life in Dharwad India. I may have lived a few miles away on the other side of the Delaware River, but I soon learned that I was far from being prepared to meet this challenge. After two months, I realized that I had failed. I could not even teach a class of elementary school children. Perhaps this realization was the biggest change in my personal and professional life. What skills did I really have and what would I do next? I was really not part of the social and political change happening in 1968, much as I may have thought I was prepared by my Peace Corps experience.

Civil rights were becoming the battle cry for disenfranchised Americans across the political spectrum. Bobby Kennedy and Martin Luther King were seen by many as martyrs for this cause. The doors were opening wider for better educational opportunities for disenfranchised children who had little or no access to our elementary and secondary schools, and educational institutions in general. President Kennedy's successor, Lyndon Baines Johnson, was a champion of this cause as well. One program area was focused on providing educational services to children with disabilities wherever they were. In the lake sixties, these children were primarily placed in institutional and special school settings with a very small minority in the "regular" school environment. My first teaching assignment after the disastrous months in the Philadelphia began in March of the next year at the New Lisbon State Colony (as it was then called) located in the Pine Barrens of southern New Jersey. A cousin of my best high school (and lifelong) friend was teaching there and they were looking for new teachers. The students/residents of this public state facility were wards of the state, and would probably live a lifetime there. Only the most "higher functioning" residents would be selected to attend classes. I was to be their "social studies/skills" teacher who would impart knowledge that would prepare them to live in the "outside" world. In reality, both students and teacher, in my case, were being given a chance to demonstrate that they could learn and improve on their prospects for another life beyond the "colony" setting. This was a far different setting than living and working in India or in many other American public school systems at that time. Whatever it may have been, it was truly a second chance to begin teaching at home.

It was an oasis in my personal transition to a more frenetic life in the States. While we were attempting to change the lives of residents in institutionalized settlings, it gave me new possibilities to pursue a role in how American public education was changing. Education was now being seen as a civil right that could not be denied on the basis of race, color, creed, or disability. More importantly for me, it was a place where I could finally come home again, and feel that my skills and experience were needed. If I succeeded, I would be part of a larger goal of the '60s of the "Great Society" that needed to be constructed in the midst of all the political and social upheaval of that time. We were trying to help poorer nations abroad, and at home we were attempting to build the great society, while young Americans were also being conscripted and dying fighting a war in Vietnam.

Local draft boards largely determined who would be selected for military service, but there were certain exemptions for teaching or other public sector professions although these determinations were not always universally applied on a national basis. At the time I was called by my draft board to report for a preliminary physical I had left my position with the

Philadelphia Public Schools and was working as a residential counselor at the Children's Home near my family's home in southern New Jersey from late 1968 into early 1969. I did not begin my teaching duties at New Lisbon State School until March of the following year. A teaching deferment would probably have been granted if I had been teaching in New Lisbon at the time of my physical but I was not. We assembled at the Burlington City draft board office early one morning in mid-December to be driven to examination/induction site in Newark, New Jersey. I did know one or two of the potential draftees who were friends of my younger brother by three years (he eventually served as a reserve in the National Guard).

During the final physical exam at the end of my Peace Corps service in India, I was found to have "converted" during my years in India from TB negative to positive indicated by the results of the tine test. I was prescribed a year's course of medication (one a day) and told to have chest x-rays on a regular basis. I may have followed up with one additional chest x-ray over that year, but my health and increased weight gain during that time assured me that I had not contracted this debilitating disease. In any case, my selective service classification changed from 1-A to 1-Y, which was used to identify someone who could be drafted in a time of a "national emergency." Fortunately for me, the Vietnam War was not considered a national emergency at that time, but still continued to drag on through 1973. The draft was eventually repealed in 1973 and was replaced by a lottery system which theoretically allowed America's youth a better system, on a national basis, to assess their potential chances of being drafted into the American military. Eventually there would be no draft, but we continued to be involved in foreign conflicts with little or no Congressional debate.

What happened in 1968 changed my life and the life of many others. In my case I was a more passive participant, but those who were more actively involved in challenging the *status quo* wanted to make sure that things would change. Now we can share more information more quickly, more widely, and keep on moving to the next "big" event. It is a race to find it, say it, and take credit for it. Let's try to remember in order to not relive the mistakes of the past. How can we grow and make our futures more about opportunity and treasure our new technologies for what they enable us all to do, not just faster, but hopefully better with greater accessibility for those who could benefit most from it. I know that I am looking back through the prism of forty-eight years of my life, but this is how I think of 1968 and the lessons I learned from that time and the changes it made in my life.

Ray Myers When I returned to the States after my years of Peace Corps service in the summer of 1968, I thought I was now ready to "change the world" at home. My experience as a volunteer in India was awe-inspiring and left me with a naive feeling that perhaps nothing was impossible to achieve if you were dedicated and committed. I had a passion to be of service in the Third World just as President Kennedy had asked us to do. I knew that I had successfully contributed to the Peace Corps mission there. I felt confident that I could now teach in the Philadelphia public schools with no formal urban teaching experience. I did not realize that I was actually returning to another world that was perhaps more foreign to me than the one where I had spent the past two years.

For me, it was not so much a matter of finding my passion since I was very much consumed with the altruism of my experiences in India and wanted to apply my presumed teaching skills to the challenges that were facing urban U.S. schools in the late sixties. Unfortunately, the challenges were larger than I ever anticipated, and I was simply not prepared to meet them. "I could surely teach fourth and fifth graders in an elementary school in inner-city Philadelphia after teaching two years at a Teacher Training College in India," I thought. This was not to be.

I was the foreigner in the city of my birth. And I had never attended a school like this. I was raised Catholic and attended only Catholic schools before joining the Peace Corps in 1966. It was a very nurturing and supportive world in which to be raised, and led me to believe in, and follow, Kennedy's clarion call to make the world a better place. Coming back to a new America at home was the hard part.

After barely surviving two months in the Philadelphia schools, I went on to spend the remainder of my professional career in the special education and educational technology fields, which also allowed mean opportunity to be involved with international developments in these areas as well. I am very appreciative of having had the opportunity to participate in these very important educational initiatives over the course of my career (officially retired from federal service in 2014). I am still continuing to pursue these and other educational interests in my blog postings that you can find at TechtoExpress, www.raymyers1101.wordpress.com.

Clem J. Nagel

You Had To Have Been There

No one quite knew what would happen. The Washington, DC police had been mustered and posted at crucial locations along the supposed route. The fear was that all would escalate into a massive riot.

Instead, it was an event that changed my life forever.

Two hundred and fifty thousand souls showed up for this March on Washington, along with me, a rural, young man from the Midwest. I was mesmerized by being a part of such a mass of humankind. As more and more people gathered, movement began near the front steps of the Capitol. People began to flow toward the Mall and the Lincoln Memorial. I found myself walking just behind Martin Luther King, Jr.

Standing near the steps to the Memorial, we listened to songs sung by Peter, Paul, and Mary, Mahalia Jackson, Bob Dylan, Joan Baez, Odetta, and Marian Anderson. King began to speak from a prepared manuscript. At first, his speech was lackluster, not very exciting.

That was until Mahalia shouted, "Tell them about the dream, Martin!" He set aside his notes and delivered one of the most famous speeches of the 20th century. Coming alive, he thundered the words *I have a dream*.

The rest was history. It doesn't take much to trigger in me vivid recollections of that Wednesday, August 28, 1963. Memories pour forth like torrential flash floods in a desert.

I had been trying to make sense of what was happening in this time in history. All the protests, boycotts, marches, and the actual naming of racism. I so wanted to make a difference.

That day, social justice became a focus of my life.

*

Having grown up in the '50s and '60s in an all-white community, only once had I seen a person with black skin-color. He was a player on another team during a state high school basketball tournament. That team came from a town just 24 miles away from my home.

In my community, discrimination was directed at Native Americans, although we did not call it racism – or see anything wrong with either our attitude or behavior. More than once, my dad told me "Indians are animals." Some teachers cautioned us to "never touch an Indian."

After the March, as part of my seminary internship, I worked in the infamous Second Precinct of Washington. At the time it was the city's most crime-ridden area. There, I regularly met with a gang of black, junior high youth who lived in its run-down tenements.

On one day I was with the gang and a helicopter flew low overhead. It blared out "President Kennedy has been shot." The gang shouted at me, "Don't leave! Stay." They ran off, soon returning with scrapbooks filled with newspaper clippings and photos of Kennedy and Cassius Clay, their two heroes. I will never forget standing there with Oliver, Donny, Sonny, Charles, and their leader JT. Tears were shed. We hugged.

A tragedy beyond imagination.

Moving to Bemidji, in northern Minnesota, I discovered the city's gas stations charged significantly higher prices to Native Americans who lived within the Red Lake Indian Reservation, eighty miles north of town. Working with the pastors of the community's churches, an agreement was reached that parishioners would purchase all their gas at nearby Cass Lake. In three days the price gouging came to a halt.

As a campus pastor, I counseled college students who were contemplating conscientious objector status. I preached anti-war sermons. And I was instrumental in the formation of an ecumenical campus ministry in the heady times of post Vatican II.

When I moved to the Twin Cities, I helped establish the first suburban Chapter of Habitat in the United States. The Chapter, affiliated with the Minneapolis Habitat for Humanity, brought a new face to issues of housing in the broader community.

The philosophy of the time was that Habitat *builds houses only in cities.* I reminded the Board that Habitat for Humanity had its beginning near Americus, Georgia (hardly an urban environment back in 1976). I convinced Habitat's Board of Directors to allow building and rehabbing houses for single-parent families and persons of color who lived in suburban neighborhoods.

We insisted that our local Chapter of Habitat provide washers and dryers in homes, since Laundromats were rarely to be found nearby. Also, the national policy of Habitat was to not build houses with garages . . . just carports, which was counter to many suburban city codes. The saying was: *Habitat builds houses for people, not cars.* With a fair amount of ingenuity, we changed that practice too.

I became a member of the Board of Directors of the Springbrook Nature Center. One year, a campaign began to have the city "annex" the Nature Center's property with the intention of converting it into a golf course. Our garage became the "distribution center" for myriads of "Save Springbrook" signs. Years afterward, I am still greeted on the street by people who say: *You don't know me, but I've been in your garage!* The effort worked. Springbrook lives on!

I hired the first black staff person to work in a suburban Twin Cities YMCA, insisting that the color of one's skin does not disqualify one. Nor is gender pertinent. I was able to offer citywide programs in which women and girls were not only welcomed, but took a direct role in planning their programs and schedules.

In 1968, I had the opportunity to be part of the first exchange of citizens between the U.S. and the USSR. As a participant in "Pathways to Peace" conference, we were there to discuss the newly launched Salt II Treaty. Near the end of our two-week visit, the joint delegation was asked to formally present a bouquet of roses at the base of the Mother Russia Monument. As the tallest *male* in the delegation, I was designated to carry the flowers along the long walk to the monument. I insisted the bouquet be divided in half, so that the tallest *female* in the procession would also have the honor. My request was granted.

Now my passion is to help others find their own voices. I teach poetry and writing in a variety of settings. I especially enjoy teaching in senior-living residences where there are many eager, enthusiastic, and talented writers! Actually, they teach me more than I could ever teach them!

I have always loved streams and rivers. Growing up in western Minnesota's Red River Valley, its rivers were important for me. As a child, I spent a lot of time sitting on the river bank, watching where two rivers, the Ottertail and the Bois de Sioux, merged to form the beginning of the Red River of the North.

The Red River is the only river in North America that journeys due north into Canada, emptying into Lake Winnipeg. More than once I have wondered if I saw in the Red River of the North, a call and a beckoning . . . urging me to move in unorthodox ways throughout my life.

Some years ago, I wrote the following poem, published in my first book *Prairie Sky Prairie Ground*.

Fear and Liberation near the Beginning of the Red River of the North

We promised never to go near
the railroad tracks—
hoboes would take us
away somewhere.

We promised never to go near
the river—
quicksand and treacherous
currents would take us
away somewhere.

We promised never to
marry a Catholic—
they wanted to overrun the world
and we would
lose our children.

We promised all this
and more,
did it all—and
        went
              away
                  somewhere.

Clem Nagel is a published poet, who began writing poetry when his poetic voice simply "showed up." His abiding interests include the diversity of other cultures, travel, spirituality, and social justice—all of which are an inseparable part of his writing. A lifelong student of the natural world, he is formally trained in theology, spiritual direction, and zoology.

He loves teaching others to be attentive to the natural environment around them and helping them find their own poetic voice. He has worked as a community organizer on a variety of efforts to improve services for people and to address social justice issues. He helped form the first suburban chapter of Twin Cities Habitat for Humanity and currently is a member of the Springbrook Nature Center Foundation.

He has published five books of poetry

Elizabeth Nagel

When I Did the Math

After the birth of my second child, my time was filled with little ones. What a gift to see the world through their eyes. I remember the day one of my children discovered she had a shadow. In the winter, my children insisted we stick out our tongues and let snowflakes land. And the proud look on my older daughter's face when she presented me with a bouquet of dandelions.

Growing up in the fifties in a rural Midwest town, marriage and motherhood were girls' intended life's vocation. My mother often said *the finest thing a woman can do with her life is bring out the best in her man.* And I was to raise his children.

Then one day I did the math. I discovered my mother had lied to me! I would be forty-five when my two children went away to college. With half my adult life stretching out before me, I said to the walls of my home: *What ever will I do all day?*

In my senior year in high school, I became a National Merit Scholarship finalist. My father advised me what to write in my essay. I was to be enthusiastic about my eagerness to marry and have children. My father said *they* would never believe me if I wrote about any secret dreams harbored in my heart. Neither my father nor anyone else ever knew any of those dreams. I loved debate and yearned to be a lawyer. It was not something a girl could achieve. And the only lawyers I knew were men.

Even after being awarded this prestigious honor, my parents' choice of college was the small, local junior college—attached to what used to be called a trade school. When the principal found out what college I was going to, he shrieked that I couldn't go there. I looked furtively down the hall, hoping no one had heard him.

Being caught between the principal and my parents put me in the odd position of defending my parents. I explained that both my parents believed the purpose of going to college for girls was not about getting an education or preparing to work. It was a back-up plan, in case something happened to their husbands.

I was a good first child. I complied with their choice of a junior college and continued to live at home. When I got phone calls from college recruiters (despite my enthusiasm for marriage and motherhood), I never told my parents. It was clear what was expected of me.

But I did an end run around my father and mother and outsmarted them! It was the Sputnik era and the sciences were big and important. So I chose to major in chemistry since my parents had no idea what chemists did. With the support of faculty and scholarship aid, I was able to transfer to a university when I became a junior.

I will never know how much that has happened in my life has been a matter of luck—or the happenstance of being in the right place at the right time. Or if my choices drew on some inner determination to not be defined by the voices of others.

I have been told that as a child a favorite phrase of mine was *I can do it myself!* Perhaps my feisty grandmother, who never went to school and lived with us until I was almost four, gave me an unexpected inheritance. She learned to read only because my grandfather patiently taught her what words on the printed page meant. My mother told me many times that I was *just like my grandmother* and she did not mean it as a compliment.

Earning my bachelor's degree was the first major threshold I crossed toward a very different life. This degree, with its unorthodox major for a girl of that time, led me into a series of life-changing events.

After college graduation, I married my childhood sweetheart. My new husband and I ran away by moving halfway across the country. Neither of us wanted to live under parental expectations. We would have gone even further if we could, but we would have fallen off the continent into the ocean.

We rented an apartment in the District of Columbia. My husband began graduate school and I "walked into" a job at the National Institutes of Health. There I was fortunate to work in the lab of a male MD, who saw me as colleague rather than technician. It was thrilling to see my name as second author on journal articles. Most bachelor degree chemists at the NIH were not treated this way. It was a dream job.

Yet voices from my childhood tugged hard. As soon as we could afford to begin our family, my first child was born. I never expected to be employed "outside the home." I walked away from all these opportunities to go further as a physical biochemist.

Now I just shake my head at what I did.

As a new mother, I tried hard to make a fulfilling life for myself. *I tried really hard.* But when my two children grew out of infancy, I did the math. At mid-life, I would have no children to parent and a busy professional husband working long hours.

This realization shook me to the core. It did not take a college degree to know that dusting, doing laundry, and reading *Better Homes and Gardens* to find new and delicious recipes would never adequately fill my days!

After much soul-searching, I applied and was accepted to graduate school to earn a doctorate in biochemistry. My plan was to create a radically different life when my two children would be in grade school and gone for the day. It was a huge step to take for a *girl* who had been programed to be an at-home wife and mother. *Girl?* I must have been at least thirty years old before I could think of myself as a woman.

However, five years away from the NIH *had changed me.* By the time I was almost done with my doctoral coursework, I made another decision. The familiar world of a biochemistry lab was no longer enough. I was more interested in the lives and cultures of most of the other graduate students, who came from countries across Southeast Asia.

Using the umbrella of being a student in the university's graduate school rather than in a particular department made it easy to move from one area of study to another. All I needed was the approval of a professor in another department. I found that professor, a man who had grown up in the Philippines for whom English was his second language. And I was admitted to a new department.

My transfer was into the prestigious psychology department, a department more selective than the medical school. I'd never have been admitted if it had been my first choice in graduate school because I had no undergraduate courses in psychology. Here I could follow my curiosity about people.

When this professor became one of my two graduate advisors, I got an added bonus. He knew his English grammar better than most people born in this country. And I, who as a chemistry major, never having written as much as a term paper, received many working versions of my dissertation covered with his red pencil.

I know he looked at my history and saw me as a future research psychologist. But my intention was the practice of psychology. Later I discovered many of my classmates took the same path in order to be admitted. On their applications to the department, they waxed eloquent about doing research—while their career aspirations were to work in clinics, community mental health centers, or hospitals.

Shades of my father's advice when I wrote my essay for the National Merit Scholarship—be enthusiastic about getting married and having children. Know your "audience" and give them what you think they want to hear. In one sense, my father was right. Bad advice I converted into a liberating future.

Neither my mother nor my mother-in-law took seriously my going to grad school. I think they believed I was just filling time until another baby arrived. I wrote to my mother when I completed my doctorate, excited about my news. She was horrified. Instead of congratulations, she called me a "disgrace to womanhood." And a number of other things not fit to say in public. I burned her letter.

The last five years of my mother's life, she saw I was doing good things as a professional person. Of course when she would come to stay with us, my home was dusted, the laundry was done, and I'd become a better cook than she ever had been.

During my graduate work and after graduation, I met other women unwilling to fill the traditional roles our generation had been taught. Together, we plotted to change the professional psychology community in our state. It was an "old boys club"—one that excluded some of their male colleagues as well as women. We were successful. Women became committee members. We were involved in making decisions affecting all of us. We got better jobs and better pay.

One unexpected experience of my professional life was becoming a committee chair in which all of the other members happened to be men. I was an "alpha male!" My colleagues expected me to tell them what we should be doing. Not my idea of how any committee should function! It took a year to transform the group's dynamics into sitting around the table as equals and making decisions about what issues we needed to address. It was the closest I came to knowing what it was like to be a *male* professional person.

I thrived in the tumultuous climate of the seventies and eighties. I found other leadership opportunities with the support of my women colleagues. It was a heady time. I was helping create new ways of being for both woman and men.

After passing my state psychology boards for licensure as a psychologist, I broke more norms. As a commentary of the times, only six women in my state saw clients privately—and three of those women were employed full-time elsewhere. I established a successful private practice, breaking more ground for women in psychology.

One of those instances of *being in the right place at the right time* was the opportunity to teach as an adjunct professor at a Protestant theological seminary (in addition to my private practice). It was something for which I had no credentials other than a doctorate in psychology. I had neither a theological degree nor was I ordained.

However, Protestant women were flocking to seminaries to act on *their* previously forbidden calls to ordained ministry. The seminary had an urgent imperative to quickly add female faculty to what had been exclusively a male domain. And I was the beneficiary. I was not about letting a few rules stand in my way.

Again, it was a dream job. This time I did not walk away and spent the next seventeen years teaching there. I was excused from working on committees, the bane of college professors. I had small classes ranging from fifteen to thirty students. I could design my own courses and create new ones. By some odd quirk, courses in pastoral care were electives (later such courses were required). Students enrolled because they wanted to take the classes I taught rather than just fulfill degree requirements.

After three decades of practice as a licensed psychologist, I took another step. I wanted to exercise some creative gifts that had remained fallow within me. When finances allowed me to step away from psychology, I closed my practice and embarked on another profession. More self-definition coming *from within me*, rather than filling some role scripted by others.

It was a hard decision. I loved listening to others as they struggled for their *own versions of self-definition*. Someone once said the reason psychotherapy works (or "talk therapy") is finding words for what is undefined inside of oneself, then expressing those issues coherently to another person. I listened and watched clients change their lives in ways they never expected. But there was not enough time during the day to do everything I wanted to do.

Not surprisingly, the power of words—such an essential part of humanity—was a precursor to this next chapter of my life. I chose to become a poet and a writer.

I expected to hit the ground running with a manuscript requiring further work. However, a weeklong workshop with a prominent fine arts nature photographer resulted in not writing a single word for almost a year. Instead, I experimented with camera and landscape.

Now I understand how unconscious wisdom within me knew what was necessary. After years of left-brain cognitive writing, with the added "burden" of psychological qualifiers, I had a lot of baggage to unlearn. Phrases like *the client is likely to . . . the client exhibits tendencies toward . . . the client may . . .* . After all, humans are complicated creatures and even for experienced professionals, predicting what someone might do at some future date is tricky business.

The year with my cameras and lenses pushed me into a nonverbal visual world. You don't "explain" photographs. They need to speak for themselves. When I emerged from that time, I wrote from my heart and my soul, not from my head.

I was granted a bonus I did not expect. Playing with visual images opened doors to exhibit my photography in juried art shows, use my photos on book covers, and to publish a book of photographs and poetry with my husband-colleague. Story of my life—go with the unexpected and see where it takes me into unexpected places.

My first love is writing poetry, a very different process than creative nonfiction or essays. Just as with photography, poetry begins with images, not words. Those images come from a different place in our brains than does language. Like psychotherapy, I find words to describe those images. Often the poetry I write has layers of meaning of which I am not consciously aware.

When I write nonfiction, essay, or op-ed, I begin with an idea rather than an image. I hone that idea using analytical skills acquired earlier in my life. But there is not a clear-cut boundary between prose and poetry. Sometimes I find myself moving in directions I did not originally intend. My inner voice knows more than what my "conscious" voice was planning to say.

When I write, whether op-ed, essays, commentaries on life, or poetry, my process reflects my life journey. An idea or visual image comes and simmers on some backburner in my interior. When it is ready, the words fall out onto the pages. Then I do minor editing for grammar, clarity, and misspellings.

Beginning with my early rebellion, my greatest insight has been learning to listen to my voice. Sometimes I ignore that voice—to my detriment. Within me is unconscious wisdom about who I am and who I am becoming. I have come to trust my inner voice.

No longer is rebellion my primary motivator, fighting back against the voices of others. Now I live in the freedom to go where my inner wisdom leads me. What a journey it has been. One well beyond my creative imagination. What more could I ask of life!

Elizabeth Nagel has followed her heart by bringing every work experience she has had as a physical biochemist and psychologist to her work today as a fine arts photographer, writer, and poet. Her life as a photographer began when she was twenty with inheritance of her father's manual SLR camera. Today's technological advances in digital photography give her greater latitude to experiment with the ordinary and extraordinary surrounding us.

She is intrigued by the interplay of color, form, and light. Much of her work includes either landscapes or close-ups that evoke the sacred. Her photographic images of the natural world breathe with the essence of who we are and invite us into layers of mystery and silence. Some of her photos come from places around the world while others are created close to home. These same themes are evident in her writing.

She has published seven books of poetry and nonfiction prose.

Robbie Orr

Three Days that Shook My World

Sam Cooke was right, when he sang "a change is gonna come,"
Though you never know when or what it will be,
It might be a hard rain that washes scales from your eyes,
Or a soft kiss of wind that blows open your mind,
Sometimes it's the dawn of a new day that changes everything.

[I]

It was a cool November morning in 1963, cool for western India that is. I was eleven, it was our long vacation and as usual I was sleeping in. The hands on the black and white clock read 8:45. Surprised to see my parents still at the dining room table, I mumbled good morning, slipped into my chair and poured myself some tea.

Instead of reading their Bible and morning prayer book my missionary parents were standing next to the shortwave radio. Through the static I could make out that a helicopter had gone down in Kashmir, killing the top generals in the Indian Army. And the President was dead. Was it a coup? Were the Pakistanis

151

or the Chinese attacking India again? My parents were very upset and tried to explain what was going on but to be honest I didn't really pay attention. I was trying to recapture my dream. Sgt. Rock and I had discovered a German Panzer column sneaking through a pass to attack American HQ. We disabled the first four tanks with grenades and trapped the whole column so it could be destroyed by P-51 Mustangs.

My father said something, then glanced at his Seiko wristwatch and rushed off to teach his 9 AM class. My mother, a nurse, rushed to the dispensary and a long line of patients. Alone I drank strong sweet tea, cut my toast into thin strips and dipped them into soft-boiled egg. It was Saturday and that meant new comics were at the English bookstore near the railway station. I finished breakfast, hopped on my bike and raced through the mission compound gate. I pedaled fast toward the Post Office when suddenly our mailman stepped into my path with a raised hand. I braked hard and skidded on the gravel.

"American-baba, such a sad day for America and for India too," He said touching his heart. I was surprised to see tears but had no idea what he was talking about so I nodded and quickly pedaled past him.

Outside the State Bank, Mr. Pandre, the guard, had a shotgun on his shoulder, a bandolier across his chest and a betel nut stained mustache that reached his ears. He gave me a big sweaty, tobacco-smelling hug.

"*Array*, Jamie-baba, why did God allow such a good man to be murdered?" Mr. Pandre was an elder at the Christian Church but the Hindu bank manager and his Muslim assistant also came running out of their office and down the steps with their arms open wide. I stepped back to avoid more hugs as they shook my hand, daubed tears out of their eyes with checkered handkerchiefs and offered their sympathy.

Similar scenes continued as I rode along the dusty main road, dodging dogs and kids in school uniforms. I passed a long line of bullock carts loaded down with sugar cane and swerved away from a big red and yellow State Transport bus. People I never knew stopped me and told me how sad and shocked they were. They really loved the first American President to visit India. I began to put it together: President Kennedy had been killed.

When the Bombay papers came later that day I read everything I could about the assassination. The next week when the Asian edition of *Time Magazine* arrived, I read it cover to cover. Kennedy's death changed everything. Kids that used to shout rude names as I rode by now waved and happily shouted "American!" And every Indian home we went to had a new picture of JFK next to those of Gandhi and Prime Minister Nehru.

In India in 1963 being an American was a pretty good thing.

[II]

Years later, on Thanksgiving Day 1969, I began to see another side of being American. It was the day when the war came home for me.

Home was the district town of Sangli in western India where my parents were medical and technical missionaries. The Vietnam War seemed far away yet the Draft grew closer every year. It was like a thunderstorm crossing the prairie. When it's far away you look at it with mild interest. As the clouds grow darker and lightning streak down you hope it will pass to the south. You see strong winds shake trees and flatten young corn in the farm across the valley. Then the light turns a sickening shade of green and mammary clouds reach for the earth. A funnel shatters a barn and sucks the pieces into the sky and you know you better run for cover.

The Draft was the storm cloud on our horizon. On the far off day when you turned 19 the sky was going to fall. As a kid you played cowboys 'n Indians or GI's vs. the Japs. By the time you were 13 you started to hear about the War. At seventeen you might know someone who'd been flattened by its winds but it still it wasn't very important, not like girls, grades, friends or sports. Then you turned eighteen. Your next birthday could bring dark clouds reaching down for you. Then you would have to decide. Were you going to run for shelter or face the storm and serve your country by resisting an un-American war or going to Vietnam? We all had to choose sides.

I used to say that good Americans should fight for their country but America was far from the dusty plains of western India where my parents worked and farther still from the missionary boarding school in the high hills of the south. If you walked around our campus it could have been a school in Cody, Wyoming instead of Kodai, South India. We'd heard about anti-war protestors but they were like alien beings; it was incomprehensible why anyone would hate America so much.

Then we heard that Dan Jackson deserted from the Navy. Dan was one of our heroes; he held a half dozen track and field records. He grew up riding a pontoon boat on muddy jungle rivers in Kerala as his Dad held revival meetings. Dan joined the Navy and volunteered for Vietnam. There he drove gun boats up and down the Mekong blasting away at Communists. Why would *he* desert?

A few days before Thanksgiving an Indian friend showed me a leftist rag called *Blitz*. It was a scandal sheet filled with anti-American propaganda interspersed with pictures of Bollywood starlets in scanty clothing. The front page had a graphic photo of dead women and kids supposedly killed by Americans but I knew that was a lie. I couldn't wait for *Time Magazine* to arrive so I could prove him wrong.

On Thanksgiving morning, I finished breakfast and took off for a bike ride before it got too hot. I drove through the busy town, dodging State Transport buses and overloaded lorries hauling sugar cane. I rode down to the Krishna River to have a smoke. The brown river water swirled along a bathing *ghat* (steps) where women did their laundry and men washed water buffalos. Little boys scrambled onto the big beasts and jumped off screaming into cool, muddy waters. Tonight was Thanksgiving Dinner. The half-dozen American families in the area were gathering at our house. There would be mounds of fried chicken and mashed potatoes with gravy, fresh rolls and maybe even a ham, with pies and cakes for desert.

Time usually arrived on Thursdays so I raced back home. Towering black clouds gathered in the sky. As I reached the mission compound a tidal wave of wind bent the tall cork and neem trees lining the soccer pitch next to our house. Heavy drops of rain splattered hard against my back as I pumped across the bumpy field. I barely made it to the house when hail rattled across the Bangalore tile roof like machine guns. I took *Time* magazine and headed for my bedroom.

There, on the cover in full color was the same picture as in that Commie rag. WHY? Women and kids in black pajamas and a blood-spattered water buffalo lay dead in a muddy lane. It could have been the people I saw at the river. They were all shot by American soldiers. HOW? Outside a fierce gust of wind shook a flame-of-the-forest tree. A large branch cracked and fell to the ground but it just missed our house. I went back to my magazine and re-read every article about My Lai. It didn't make sense. Americans didn't do that kind of thing but these American soldiers *had* killed women and kids. It was in *Time* so it must be true.

Had Dan Jackson seen anything like that? Was that why he deserted? A sick feeling rose in my gut. Next year I would turn 19. Would I go to Vietnam?

That evening the missionaries gathered around the table and offered thanks. Platters of chicken, mashed potatoes and rich brown gravy were served but I couldn't eat a bite. My stomach was turning and in every spoonful I saw a bone that would stick in my throat, a jagged bone in the shape of Vietnam.

[III]

On a soft spring day in in Iowa everything changed again. It was my sophomore year at Grinnell College; the finger of the

Draft had passed over me, thanks to a lucky lottery number. The Nixon Administration was negotiating an end to the long war. American troops were pulling out and South Vietnamese were taking over.

That day didn't actually start well. I had a thundering headache from partying the night before. I had to study for two big tests—macro-economics and statistics—on the same damn day. Outside the window of our apartment the sun shone brightly. I winced and made coffee in the dingy kitchen. My roommates had left a stack of dirty dishes in the sink and remnants of *The Des Moines Register* on the table. I sorted through ads and sports pages looking for the news section. I wasn't much of an activist but I had to read about the War each morning; every evening I was in the student lounge watching Walter Cronkite tell it like it was.

NIXON BOMBS HANOI

In big bold 68-point type, *The Register* riveted my brain. Hot bolts of metal shot through me as I read about the Hanoi railway station, schools, hospitals and homes all swept away by a rolling wave of destruction as B-52s carpet bombed North Vietnam.

Secretary of State Kissinger was quoted, "We have to force the Communists to negotiate seriously."

And it wasn't just Hanoi. They were mining Haiphong harbor that was full of Russian and Chinese ships. If one of them blew we could be facing fucking WWIII.

I gulped my hot coffee, grabbed a backpack of books and raced downstairs for my bike. I had to get to campus and see what was happening. There hadn't been demonstrations at Grinnell since the 1970 strike over the invasion of Cambodia and murders of four students at Kent State, all of which I'd missed. Still there were lots meetings or movies or speakers on the War. Last week the American Friends Service Committee had brought their Tiger Cage exhibit to campus. It exposed the grotesque torture chambers the South Vietnamese government ran on Con Son Island; your American tax dollars at work. The terror bombing of the cities was sure to set off a huge wave of protests. Finally the anti-war movement would come back to life and this time I could be part of the solution. Together we would all make a real difference.

The sky was an Iowa spring blue and a wonderful 65 degrees. I rushed to the student union and looked around. No one was handing out leaflets, no notices of meetings or demos on the billboards. People sat around drinking coffee. A big radical on campus sat with his girlfriend reading the *New York Times* and eating bagels. I took a deep breath and asked how Grinnell students should respond to the bombing.

"Yeah, it's pretty fucked up, man," He mumbled as he folded his paper and stood up. "I'll check with the Committee. We'll figure out what to do. I got some business to take care of now."

"The Committee? Who is that?"

He looked at the blonde woman and jerked his head toward the door. "Let's go to the meeting."

"No way, how can we get high while they're bombing schools and hospitals." She turned to me. "What do you think?"

I looked at the former SDS leader. He shrugged and walked away.

Me? What did I think? What were the radicals going to do? They were the leaders, not me. I couldn't believe they were going to go get high. I was just a confused, scared, angry kid. Sure, like the rest of my generation I'd watched people sit-in at lunch counters, ride segregated Greyhounds, get beaten by brutal cops. And they did change the world of Jim Crow. But they were activists …heroes, not a skinny white kid like me.

I sat down with the blonde woman who was smiling at me as if I might actually know something and we talked. We talked about terror bombing of civilians and how we each became aware of the War, about the System we lived in. Follow the money, her lawyer mom always told her. Wars were always caused by money or power.

"Let's find other people ready to take action," Johanna said. "I bet Women's House will help."

We left the cafe talking rapidly. Her boyfriend and the rest of his "Committee for Third World Liberation" were playing Frisbee on the lawn. Other students were sunbathing, walking to Burling Library or studying under trees like it was just another day. No one seemed to care. It was unreal.

I flashed back to TV footage—a wave of exploding earth swept across a field, engulfing a school. I could see B52s carpet-bombing Grinnell College; the Fine Arts Center exploding and a wave of destruction swallowing South Campus. I felt sick to my stomach and leaned against a tree.

"Johanna," someone called out. Several women and a Puerto Rican guy with a big afro approached us. "We gotta figure out what to do about the fucking bombing!"

We sat on the grass and talked and cried and raged. The War of our lives was *not* winding down. All the hope and fear and anger of the Sixties were riding shotgun in the sky battling in the dark way beyond the blue, way above those fluffy, prairie clouds. What could a handful of students do? How could we change a world that was poisoned with Agent Orange and DDT, where our government terror-bombed civilians just like the Nazis at Guernica, where people died in ghettoes years after Martin Luther King himself was shot, and where women were getting raped and killed every day? How could five students make a difference when no one else cared?

"How about a hunger strike?" Roberto, the guy with the 'fro, suggested. "Like Cesar Chavez."

"Yeah," Johanna replied. "A hunger strike will get people's attention. We should all camp out in Herrick Chapel; the chapel as our strike headquarters will create a different tone."

Roberto and Johanna had sparked something in each of us, something new and deep; it wasn't just outrage at the War. Exhilaration shone in our eyes; there was hope and a vision that a better world *is* still possible. And we could help it arrive. We committed to fast for at least one week. We'd drink juice but no solid foods or alcohol. During the week we hoped to attract a few others and together we'd figure out what to do. At cafeteria dinner lines we passed out leaflets asking anyone who cared about the terror-bombing to join us in Herrick Chapel. Then we went back to our rooms to get sleeping bags.

By the time I got to the chapel 900 students had joined us. We weren't alone anymore.

I walked to the chancel to join my new friends who stood staring at the crowd. The aisles were jammed and the balcony was overflowing. Towering stained glass windows, plush red carpet and hundreds of faces gave off a warm glow. Voices blended quietly into a low buss that reverberated off the vaulted ceilings.

"What do *we* do now?" I whispered to Johanna.

She looked at me, eyes filled with light. "I don't know but *WE* just got a whole lot bigger!"

Since then I've known that even a skinny kid (or a balding, old man) can always make a difference.

Robbie Orr The fast at Grinnell College turned into a week of anti-war protests in the small Iowa town. As part of wave of anti-war activity across the country, it culminated in a national student strike and a large demonstration at the Iowa State Capitol in Des Moines. Personally Orr found community, a sense of purpose and freedom within the anti-war movement. Born and raised in India as the son of Scottish and American missionaries, Robbie used his inherited zeal in his newly found mission of radical socialism.

Politically the U.S. Government ended the draft and abandoned the War in Vietnam because of unprecedented resistance at home and the unraveling of the Armed Forces. The Civil Rights Movement became the struggle for Black Power and began to disintegrate from police repression and internal conflict. The Women's Movement was changing the face of America but it probably was more successful at personal than political change. By the mid-seventies the chaotic movement for social change was dissipating. Robbie and his companions looked for ways to keep the movement going and turned to Marxism for answers.

Moving to St. Paul in 1975, Orr became involved in the Coop Wars and was attracted by the logic of a secretive group called the Coop Organization. It recruited dedicated Euro-American activists but was led by a Black man who had worked with James Foreman in SNCC. His purported plan was to develop a woman-led organization to build cooperative groceries, garages, daycare centers and clinics. The CO became more and more hierarchical and secretive and eventually turned into a full-fledged cult. Orr survived to return to activism and is writing a series of novels, *The Repentant Radical Trilogy*. The first novel includes the vignettes in this essay. The working title is called *Sea Chains* and Robbie Orr is shopping it around.

Laurence Peters

Belonging

"There is always one moment in childhood when the door opens and lets the future in. We should be thankful we cannot see the horrors and degradations lying around our childhood, in cupboards and bookshelves, everywhere." — Graham Greene

London, England 1960

I am eight or nine. It is another dreary day of the school holidays. It's a long afternoon, one that found me lost in its deep subterranean weeds. When would its relentless boredom end, when would I swim free of the day's cloudy aquarium glow?

Same old questions, who was I? Who were these parents of mine? What was I doing here? What could I do to turn this experience of staying home and having time float over me into something vaguely interesting?

I was sitting staring at my reflection in front of my mother's dresser window, in my parents' bedroom. On one side of me was the large pharaohs' tomb-like wardrobe looking down on me in judgment. A wardrobe that had been there since creation, with its somber heavy wood, it could have made an ocean voyage and kept us all safe; it was now humbled as my memory palace preserving my mother's gigantic fur coat and long brocaded dresses, my father's best double-breasted suits, and an assortment of hats—dark velvet for her and smooth felt wide brimmed for him. As a small child I had often squeezed my way into its dark interior, tolerating the suffocating moth-ball smell for a chance to rub my skin against the space's exotic textures. As I got older, I took out some of the clothes and imagined their glory days when they traveled about town hailing taxis in the rain. It had become one of my rituals to see how long I could stay inside the enormous clothes museum and hide for a while. They never seemed to miss me but there was at least one reward—air never smelled as sweet as it did when I was rid of its ancient clutches.

But today what caught my attention was the twin chest of drawers supporting the dresser mirror like two wooden soldiers. Something told me that there were riches to explore here also and the risks of possibly getting found out were worth it. I had known for some time that there were photographs of my parents and their families buried deep here and some letters, but having rifled through them once or twice for who knows what, I had never thought to read them. After all many of the photos were dark and faded and the handwriting on most of the letters was, to my semi-literate eyes, impossible to read. But suppose I tried harder this time. Maybe there was something more that could be revealed. I searched for a spot I knew well; there deep inside the lower left hand drawer was a tin chocolate box secured by rubber bands. There they were again waiting for me, but as I tried reading them again, noticing that the letters were addressed from the US. It occurred to me that the love letters in blue aerograms that I first thought were all from my dad because they were signed with my father's first name, were from some other man also named Ben like my father. Could there have been two Bens in my mother's life? This new Ben, it

162

appeared, was an American GI and he hailed from upstate New York, not from London England. The letters were full of odd expressions like "my honey" and my "English rose" and with a longing that even from my nine or ten-year-old perspective appeared deep and heartfelt.

Interspersed with the letters were postcards of some American landmarks. I remember the Empire State, Yellowstone National Park, and many large Greco-Roman buildings surrounded by green verdant lawns bathed in golden sun, and the U.S. Congress building. They were odd, not like any postcards I had ever seen. They were half photo and half an artistic rendering using a palette of colors that were taken from a Disney cartoon or a fish tank. The blues were a chemical never-to-be-realized blue; the green's close to aquamarine. The astonishing perspectives and unreal color combinations created a Wizard of Oz unreality to the scene that made it all the more fascinating for my young brain cells to conjure with. I returned to those dream-like images often trying to place them in the world I knew. They did not fit. Everything about them suggested that this new world was built along different principles according to different measurements. After a while I grew tired and returned the letters as best as I could to their neat home inside a tin chocolate box.

I know I must have said one or two things to my mother asking her about the American who seemed in love with her. She did not seem to have minded that the source of the information had been contained inside the drawer, and she laughed it off as a youthful romance that had been forgotten for a long time. My father had been her true love, but she made it clear that she had considered his marriage offer that would have involved her moving like so many GI brides to the States. When later, as I began to put some of the pieces together, the story she had told me had been largely correct. Evacuated out of London she lived with her parents near a U.S. Air Force base in Oxford. There were plenty of socials so that the American GIs could find eligible English brides who were considered by the visiting Yanks as hot property since they were viewed as better homemaker material than their more assertive American counterparts. It was in this manner that her younger sister had been swept off her feet by an American and made her way to New York's Long Island. She had been tempted to do the same but seeing the heartbreak that her sister's rapid departure from England had caused her parents, she decided to hold off and during this time she met my father who really did fall in love with her. But those pictures remained in my mind somehow along with the romance of a country that seemed to be living in color while we in post-war-austerity Britain lived in black and white. It was always a question that was left hanging for her about what would have happened had she never met my dad or had made an impulsive decision at a tender age to join her sister. The pictures haunted me and offered to my young self a dreamscape, another world that was exotic, romantic and different from the mundane every day of my youth and my conventional surroundings.

September 1978, Ann Arbor, Michigan

It's 7:45 AM. I am walking across the Big M Michigan diag. Students are already on the move, some teeming out of these large classical buildings, some wearing shorts, some sweatshirts, and some in hoodies. All heading somewhere. They have 15 minutes to find their new classes. I have not yet registered for any but know first I must teach my opening section of Freshman English, introduce myself, check that they purchased the three texts they were required to read: a rhetoric guide to English Composition, a Freshman English reader, and Strunk and White. Students are first-semester eager and ready to take their seats, wanting to find out what this college life is like. I am moving to another giant building, an old gymnasium to get registered for fall classes, carrying a large catalog, dog-eared with my preferences marked in ink, ready to be transferred to some kind of IBM card full of slots and holes that could be chewed up by a computer and organize my semester.

There they are—the first American students I am going to teach, the class that meets every Tuesday and Thursday at 8 AM. The students stare mournfully back at me, looking to judge from every gesture I make just how difficult the class is going to be and how many shortcuts they can take. We went around the room as I asked the largely all-white and blond group, most dressed in down jackets, some in go blue sweatshirts and an odd couple of guys in shorts although it was freezing out, what they were studying (their majors) and their career goals. Many just said business or engineering. A few wanted to be lawyers and one wanted to be a doctor. Most came from small towns in Michigan, but a few came from New York and New Jersey. For the first class they all wanted to put the best face on it, but it was clear that the majority were less than enthusiastic to be there since many of their brighter peers had "placed out" of freshman English by doing well on a test. But good troopers that they were, they saw the class as another one of those ticket-punching things they had to do to get what was promised to them. A nice middle-class education with a middle-class paycheck at the end. I dutifully took roll and told them about my mandatory office hours in my cubicle.

As doctoral students and freshman English teaching fellows we had to toe the party line when it came to teaching English. It was all about the students being able to master certain kinds of "rhetoric"—the five-paragraph essay, but it was never called that as it sounded too simple. Instead, it was called transactional writing and it had its own "grammar." Personal writing about issues you cared about was sort of beside the point, valued for the purposes of recording your thoughts in a daily journal but otherwise optional. Good writing was about mastering a certain rhetorical technique which you could distill from analyzing the work of prose masters like E. B White and J.L. Mencken. It was not an approach I could readily accept as it made teaching English more like teaching a foreign language than a way to express oneself. It went against my own training as well, which was to help students develop a personal voice through writing about themes and experiences they were familiar with and to enjoy sharing their work with an audience.

Although I tried to give them exercises from their textbooks and the handouts that would invariably have them complete paragraphs that were missing topic sentences and supportive detail, I diverged a few weeks into the semester into stuff that interested me more and that could get me excited about teaching a course that began at the god-awful hour of 8:00 in the morning. I found some good essays from "the Reader"—a telephone directory-sized expensive volume that came along with the slightly less large but more expensive "the Rhetoric" that had some good essays by authors like James Baldwin and Toni Morrison among more stodgy ones. Despite my encouragement, less than half usually completed the reading leading to the same dismal hurried discussions where someone who had read the text did a content summary and the rest just listened. I spent the hours in my cubicle correcting papers and making sure that my comments were not too discouraging, giving out A's and A-'s for B+ and B- work.

Some came to conferences on a regular basis. Their high school careers had prepared them to be brown-nosers. Brian Friedman showed up one afternoon, lifting his large backpack over his puffy down jacket. He took a moment to ask me about my background and his memories of visiting London, and then quickly got to the point by telling me point blank that the B I had given him was "unacceptable" and unless I gave him an A in the course I was jeopardizing his chances to go to medical school. "What did he have to do to earn an A?" he said in the most charming and insistent manner. He needed to go to medical school and knew that unless he got an A- his career goal was in jeopardy and I was standing in his way. I thought he was overdramatizing and exaggerating but felt that he could at least be given the chance to rewrite some and perhaps write for what was called "extra credit. What was at stake here? Not a whole lot. My ego, my sense of authority were not quite as strong as some of the instructors who saw themselves as some kind of academic gatekeepers ensuring the unwritten rules around academic norms and how much they could be bent. But that was what the office hours stuff seemed all about: helping those who had mastered the skills of negotiation to practice their skills on young and vulnerable TAs who also knew that an unfavorable end of semester review could also negatively affect their own careers. While I forgot what his problem was— probably a lot of wooden sentences and not enough detail—I did get to know the issues one of our few Hispanic students was having: her inability to write a cogent English sentence. We went through her work in painstaking detail. She too had high ambitions, I think to become a lawyer "back in my country" but there was no way with her thin grasp of English that she could pass my course, let alone the other four or five she was taking. Amazingly, few or none of the other courses required any written English. It was all true false or fill in the missing word. After going over her writing a few times, I suggested she work with a tutor.

That tactic often allowed nonstandard English speakers and minorities to stay in school while their English improved. Back then "affirmative action" was the term of the day and we all liked the notion of a diverse student body and for everyone to join the happy melting pot that soon enough was to become the multicultural salad that we called America. Everyone was on the upward escalator including my fellow baby boomers who shared the maze of cubicles—former high school and community college teachers pursuing their doctorates, including a few who fancied themselves as writers and sported interesting hats and sophisticated retro-looking clothes and even a chap from Belfast, Paul, who spoke with a thick brogue and wore black. He thought it was wonderful over here and did not want to go back. Maggie, another TA, had a crush on Paul and was writing her third volume of poetry and nicely crafted prose pieces full of careful descriptions of churchyards at dusk. She had a keen artistic soul, used her cubicle time to talk to her students, and was always good with faculty gossip having us all laughing at the absurdities of the lecherous faculty trying to hit on certain women who were all too willing to do their bidding in exchange for a prized graduate assistantship job. We all knew that if we failed to get the literature teaching job, either at a college or a university, then our lives would be doomed to bonehead English—to training dull, conformist bureaucrats by the truckload to write better memos. I did not yet know what I wanted to do. I had an American girlfriend and most of my social life was wrapped around visiting her, so I had deferred thinking about whether I would return to my life in London. This was the now and the world crowded in on me displacing any lonely or backward looking thoughts. I wanted to find something more in this experience. I wanted to try to distill what this whole American thing was about.

What I knew was that it was a pretty walled off space—a special sort of cultural oasis that allowed a predominantly white male faculty with the right combination of personal charm and performance skills to take the admiration of female graduate students to the next level or not as they so chose. While minorities were in plentiful supply among the small armies of service workers needed to clean, cook and maintain operations within the massive buildings, minority professors were a rare breed who stayed within narrow academic subspecialties or in the fields of science, technology and engineering. Occasionally these workers would rally in the quad for better pay and conditions to the embarrassment of the liberal administration. The fear was that the few black graduate students would join with them or cause some further attention to be paid to the sorry lack of diversity on the Michigan campus. Most of the African-American students in the grossly substandard Detroit schools some 50 miles away could only dream of attending this white enclave and had to content themselves either with Community College or the inner city Wayne State University or sports-oriented colleges in burned out industrial heaps like Flint, Lansing or Ypsilanti, old rusty towns that serviced rusty auto plants and prisons. Places that if you had any youth in your body you would get up and leave and never look back.

Ann Arbor was by comparison a sort of Athens for the region, richly endowed with world-class libraries and concert halls, not to mention a medical school and athletic departments. The gargantuan campus was supported by an elite set of forward-looking alumni and business leaders; it was also reluctantly and slowly trying to serve as the school's conscience after trying since its founding to establish a Midwestern Harvard, which unlike its eastern counterpart would be combined with a winning football team. Its view of the Midwest was a white Anglo view that excluded Blacks and Hispanics in vital ways.

A growing group of African-American students and civil rights activists wanted the university to move faster on an affirmative action agenda—more courses that addressed the world from minority perspectives to balance out the almost absurd emphasis on the European cultural heritage. Taking a page from the women's rights movement, they wanted a curriculum that reflected more of the African-American experience and more "affirmative action" as far as recruiting Black students from inner city Detroit schools who mostly failed to ever think of applying to the great U of M since they viewed the school as a white enclave.

My ears pricked up when my friend Cheryl—herself a representative of Michigan's changed view of itself and a Black woman from Mississippi who wanted to teach English Literature in a northern college—told me of a special program to teach freshman English to students who had graduated from inner city Detroit schools after going through a summer bridge program as seniors. I remember many of them sitting there in the room reserved for the "special program" staring back at me, some with slightly puzzled looks as they tried to follow my British accent. Most of them knew they were not quite college ready and were trying to deal with the possibility that this might be all a white man's trick.

One student who used to wear a double-breasted suit to class and a big salesman's smile on his face knew the game, and although frequently absent—it seemed there were always funerals and sick relatives to attend to that necessitated him staying in Detroit for long periods—was always coming up to me after class and wanting to talk about his papers. Perhaps he could rewrite the sentences that I had underlined as not making any sense and make sure that he got the grade he deserved. How did I tell him it did not work like that? That the issue was not just one or two sentences but a whole approach. He wanted an answer and was prepared to negotiate it all out with me there and then so we could get this all resolved neatly. He wanted me to play the game and tried to charm me into giving him the grade he wanted with more panache than dear old Brian Friedman. Fortunately, there was a ready supply of tutors who had been especially recruited to help these students.

What also helped was that I could largely dispense with the overly technical rhetorical tosh that I had been forced to teach in the first semester and work with "a Reader" that was full of great prose by African-Americans like James Baldwin writings and Martin Luther King's Letter from Birmingham Jail. The stuff still seemed not quite geared to their experience but it was a start. Their reading experience was limited to whatever experience they had been subjected to in the name of school and had left them with a respectful admiration for written words but not much sense of their own power to wield them. But get them on a topic they cared about—their family, cars, sports teams and they were off to the races.

College was another game they would figure out and get right soon. Just give them time and time is what Michigan tried to give them, but they represented a token effort that had to be carefully managed since the last thing the university wanted to become was to be a savior for the Detroit public schools. The "Harvard of the North" ideal was to attract the nation's best and brightest to campus thus increasing out-of-state tuition and satisfying wealthy alumni who would happily provide for the latest new building projects on campus.

The way that race was emerging as an issue in American life continued to fascinate me. The white liberals, whose courses I attended, were also watching to see how the issue would play out on campus and in politics generally. They had come up during the '60s and, having absorbed what both the civil rights movement and the counterculture, were prepared to sometimes take a stand to prompt the university to do more. Marvin Felheim, for example, dying of bone marrow cancer and teaching his American culture class from his hospital bed in his house across from the University's main campus, still had some acerbic things to say about the administration's lack of willingness to embrace diversity. People had urged me to take his class. He was a student favorite for unashamedly embracing popular culture and seeing that the American experience was bigger than what could be captured in novels and poetry or spilling out into films, TV, theater and even cartoons. Those who could write about the experience should not just be from the privileged white homes but should include all who could admire creativity and artistry.

He would often pose questions, his white head alert to a dozen or so of us gathered around his raised bed. "What makes baseball the quintessential American sport?" he would ask. We would all proffer an explanation. It's the most popular, the most fun. "No," he would reply. "It's because of the homerun. There are no boundaries. In every other game there is a boundary past which the game is over or someone is out. There are no boundaries for the homerun. The ball can soar out of a stadium and land in the next state. The fans are always waiting for that moonshot hit and that is why. This is a culture that aspires to the frontier." Coming from Felheim, a dyed-in-the-wool lefty, that notion of an American frontier was more than just a territorial ideal. It impressed me as did his commitment to teaching, which should be giving more of yourself to students, not just getting them to be facile readers of texts. One or two classes were cancelled when he was too sick or needed to go to the hospital, but he was a trooper and always sought to make our reading about American popular culture relevant to the present, whether it be the influence of the vaudeville tradition on popular entertainment, cowboy movies or his delight in some of his favorite TV shows, "Mary Hartman" and "Laverne and Shirley." Some of his words to us doctoral students were "Don't let them make you over. You are fine as who you are." I wanted to believe that my perspective and voice had something of value to offer and that no single view of reality should dominate.

The professors I enjoyed the most were the ones that played the game differently. Like Cliff Barratt who had the audacity to turn his seminar room into a courtroom to re-air the Ann Arbor Black English case. As a lifelong resident of Ann Arbor who had followed education politics his whole life, he was miffed that he had missed "the trial of the century" because that year he was on sabbatical to Denmark, of all places. The case was brought by eleven students whose parents believed that the students had been discriminated against by the school system as speakers of Black English. The discrimination they had suffered was varied but included being improperly referred to special education and being generally humiliated by their second-class treatment.

Barritt had the creativity to include the trial transcript as the reading and some of the expert witnesses who testified to provide their side of the story. We even went to the school and interviewed the parents and heard from the lead attorneys as well as the judge. I cannot remember much about the evening we attended the ironically named Martin Luther King Elementary School or the setting except the coldness and formality.

After so much legal wrangling, everyone was on their guard and choosing their words carefully. As I became more familiar with the case, the racial dynamics were not quite easy or as obvious. There was first an issue of how the largely Black teachers in this white school system managed to negatively discriminate against African-American children. The racial elements were hard to separate from the class issues which were both rooted in the reluctant efforts of the Ann Arbor school system to use housing policy instead of busing to desegregate the largely all white and middle class school district. By allowing only a small number of families to rent or purchase homes in a small middle class enclave, they were setting the children up for problems. The Judge rejected the plaintiffs' main claims but found that the district "failed to take into account the home language of the children in the provision of education instruction"—an apparent violation of federal law meaning that the teachers had to be subjected to professional development to enable the teachers to use Black English to help students read.

The trial left me with some mixed feelings. There was no good remedy, but at least it was possible to send a signal that for full integration to work, you needed to do more than place a few Black families in a school district and expect them to survive academically.

The longtime leftist civil rights lawyer who brought the case wanted to frame a broader constitutional argument that these poor kids were not being afforded an equal education; he could not help but be disappointed with the result. But at least it brought attention to the issue, and the African-American parents—tired of their kids failing to learn, being sent to special education, or dropping out—were now looking for other remedies in their pursuit of the good old but illusive American dream.

Law was one route, legislation another. Both of these seemed more powerful to me than puttering along pretending I was interested in teaching English Literature at some small college in the boonies. But these thoughts were slow to dawn. Working without passion at a doctoral dissertation that seemed to be leading nowhere, I grew restless for something more fulfilling—for an intervention that could make a difference.

Then sitting in an Ann Arbor Arboretum one day, term over, sunshine pouring down on a beautiful lawn and trees, I read an article in *The New York Times* under the subheading of the New Gypsy Scholars. I remember one statistic that stood out from the generally gloomy report on the practice of would-be college teachers taking three or four teaching gigs for low money or uprooting themselves every few years because one- or two-year contracts at small colleges had run out. The article went on to destroy any hopes I may have cherished for an academic career by reciting a statistic that would rebound endlessly in my head: only a one-in-ten chance of anyone getting hired for a tenure slot and then another one-in-ten chance of anyone making tenure. Those were not good odds. I needed to find something else to do with myself than pursue an idle dream of teaching at a university. Ann Arbor was already feeling like a small college town. Everything revolved around the great U of M. I was beginning to feel claustrophobic and wanting to return to the world outside of its cozy confines. But where?

Washington DC, 1987

I am sitting in an office being interviewed for a job as counsel to a Congressional Subcommittee. In front of me is Black Congressman Major R. Owens who had patiently waited for three or four terms to become a subcommittee chair after serving for a long period in the New York State Senate. He had begun life as a sharecropper's son and attended Morehouse College, the same university as Martin Luther King. He had marched with King and had run Mayor Lindsay's Community Development Agency in New York City. A stout man with a large impassive face, he is wearing a crisp dark blue suit and tie and looking at me from the comfort of a red upholstered armchair.

After allowing me to settle, he asks what made me think I would do well at this job. He sits back. He examines my expression for a moment. I try not to show fear and exude confidence, but in my mind there are many thoughts. Don't f** up. Try to stay cool. Control your words. It is all about control. I have gone through four years of law school, completed my Ph.D., taken lots of college teaching jobs and unpaid internships to be sitting here. Now, at last, the moment of truth. Phrases are bubbling up and bursting in my mind. This is the job that I wanted. I have known all along that this is a job where I can help make a difference. They all sound reasonably good but were they me? And who was I now? I had been running so fast towards some goal, but what was it? What was the finish line? Why not believe for once in something real. Take off the academic mask and connect your ideas to something real. Why not.

I begin. I want a life of purpose. Most people want not a job but a vocation, something they can feel dedicated to and become part of. I tell him about the Black English case and how these people were denied a voice but pinned their claims on a federal guarantee of equal education opportunity. Perhaps as a Brit I could be privileged to voice an outsider's view that the system had worked in a way. Although the outcome was not perfect, a start had been made. Owens must obviously believe in that power of democratic system to give a voice to the voiceless, the capacity to include more people in the fold of representative government. Although my academic insights must have seemed so insignificant to the real struggles that he had experienced coming up, we found a place we could meet. Getting that job represented the beginning of the long effort to connect, to realize the different parts of me that had whispered their existence back in my parents' bedroom all those years ago.

Postscript

At one point towards the end of her life, my mother wanted to write a book about someone who could live two lives. Do you think it could work? she asked me. I said yes, if you write it. But by that time her vision was not good and writing was a struggle, although that did not stop her trying. But then something novelistic did happen. My aunt found herself in the same store one day when she was out in her Florida retirement community where she spotted whom she identified as my mother's former beau. My dad had recently died and she had taken to visiting her sister on a more frequently in the States, so my aunt asked whether my mum would be interested in meeting him again after all these years. My aunt had found out that he had been a dentist and had developed a large practice in upstate

New York before retiring to Florida. However, she warned my mother that his vision was now failing him and he walked only with some difficulty. Mum asked me what I thought. I said there was nothing to lose and she should go and talk over old times. She was nervous and worried about how she would feel seeing him in such decline. But she went ahead with a lunch appointment and they had a good time reminiscing.

Laurence Peters   I was born in London, England and now live in a Maryland suburb that surrounds Washington DC. After teaching English and Drama at a Sixth Form College outside London, I left for the U.S. on a graduate fellowship from the University of Michigan, Ann Arbor. I studied education and became interested in how the courts could make a larger impact on the issues surrounding educational inequality, so upon completing my course work and doctorate, I enrolled in law school and a few years later became counsel to the Subcommittee on Select Education & Civil Rights for the U.S. House of Representatives (1986-1993). Subsequently I became a Clinton political appointee serving as a Senior Policy Advisor to the U.S. Department of Education (1993-2001).

My focus in Washington was on the way the federal government could bring more resources— intellectual, financial and institutional—to assisting America's inner cities. I saw technology as a potential game changer and co-wrote *From Digital Divide to Digital Opportunity* (Rowman 2003) and co-edited *Scaling Up: Lessons from Technology Based Educational Improvement* (Jossey Bass 2005), and *Global Education: Using Technology to Bring the World to Your Students* (ISTE 2009).

My book, *The United Nations: History and Core Ideas,* was published fall 2015 by Palgrave Macmillan and follows from my work as Graduate Program Director of the United Nations Association National Capital Region. It is consistent with my firm conviction that planetary survival can only be secured through countries working together to create a peaceful and sustainable future. I also have three children who I believe need to inherit a more stable planetary future. I continue to teach politics and education courses for Johns Hopkins University. www.laurencepeters.com

Roy Wolff

Be Calmed in Korea:
The Making of a Peacemaker

I have been a member of Veterans For Peace, nationally and locally, since 1985. In the 1950s I spent two years of my life in the U.S. Army, most of that time in Korea. I had arrived in Korea on a troopship after the shooting part of the war had ended, and thus became part of an "occupation" army. This was in a divided country where millions of people had been killed within three years—probably three million in North Korea, and at least half as many in South Korea. In both countries, it was mostly civilians who had been killed.

For sixteen months, my work in Korea was part of an effort to restore some semblance of order to the lives of those who had survived the war. My job was returning land and buildings that we Americans had confiscated from Korean civilians. Now we were trying to give shelter and food to hundreds of thousands of civilians who did not have the necessities of life.

These included many, many widows and orphans. Tens of thousands of orphans! I still have a lot of memories and pictures of those orphans, including photos from one orphanage where I spent Christmas Day in 1956 shortly before I rotated back to the U.S.A.

I looked, I finally really looked, into the very sad eyes of those children in that unheated building in that freezing weather, and I said to myself, "This is BULLSHIT! Warmaking is pure, unadulterated BULLSHIT, and I no longer want any part of what causes this hell on earth." On that Christmas Day, in that orphanage, I finally lost it! Lost what? I lost any desire and willingness to support any part of warmaking.

Many years later I went back to Asia to peacemaking conferences in South Korea and Hiroshima in 1995 and in North Korea in 2003. And what did I find in North Korea? People who were just as delightful as the South Koreans and just as deserving of peace. Fifty years after the end of the shooting war, some of the North Koreans still had that sad, underfed look. There's still no agreement to end the war and the division of the country.

In preparation for Armistice Day on 11-11, I start ringing a little bell in my home office every day, eleven times at about 11 AM. During and after the ringing of this small bell, I remain silent and reflective, praying or meditating on different things. Often I think about my wife, myself and our nine grandchildren, and about what my wife and I could do to work toward a better future for our children and grandchildren, and for your children and grandchildren, and for many others. I always close my meditation or quiet time by repeating words spoken by Dan Berrigan at the of Catonsville Nine trial in 1968 during the American War in Vietnam:

"The time is past when good people may be silent. How many indeed must die before our voices are heard? How many must be tortured, dislocated, starved, maddened? How long must the world's resources be raped in the service of legalized murder? When at what point will you say no to this war? We have chosen to say with the gift of our liberty, if necessary, our lives: The violence stops here. The killing stops here. The suppression of the truth stops here. This war stops here."

Be Calmed in Korea

If you want peace,   be calm.
Calmness.   Peace.
Travel light,   for the journey is short.
Cash and carry.

It was after darkness fell,
as black as faith.
Lanterns lit, they led us out of town,
out of our control.

We wanted peace.   We were calm.
It was a good night.   Irene.
We arrived at dawn.   Beyond Joy.
The Land of the Morning Calm.

The poem above and the ones that follow were written weeks after I returned from a month-long trip to South Korea and Hiroshima, Japan, in the summer of 1995. That pilgrimage took place forty years after I had served 469 days as a soldier in the U.S. Army occupation of Korea, and fifty years after an uncle of mine had helped Harry Truman decide to drop atomic bombs on Hiroshima and Nagasaki in August of 1945. I use the word *pilgrimage* because I returned to Asia at age sixty to apologize for acts of violence that my country and I had perpetrated in that region in the 1940s and 1950s. I was with a contingent of Veterans For Peace, and we and thousands of others did apologize and tried to make amends for our addiction to war-making by speaking, marching, protesting current injustices, fasting and praying at places like the Hiroshima Peace Park on the 50th anniversary of the first atomic devastation.

When I arrived home from Japan I was emotionally and physically exhausted for weeks, slept very fitfully and was often feverish with cold and flu symptoms. My doctors said that my immune system had become compromised. Webster's Dictionary lists one of the definitions of compromise as "to endanger the life or reputation by some act which cannot be recalled." Early one September morning I was trying to sleep in a spare bedroom, and while only partly awake I grabbed a nearby pen and paper and wrote down the "poem" about Korea exactly as you see it above. Once I became more alert I followed that "literary effort" with seven very short poems about incredible individuals I met in the Japan part of my journey. Most of them had walked from Auschwitz in Poland to be in Hiroshima on the 6th of August 1995.

I know that reputable poets rarely choose to clarify the words or concepts in their writings, but I feel the need to comment on a few of my wordings. "Cash and carry" is an old-fashioned phrase I use to show a need to pay up personally and to move on (a variation might be "put up or shut up"). "Irene" is the Greek word or name for Peace, and "Good Night, Irene" is a well-known folk song with a hidden meaning. Moreover, there was a girl named Irene in my past who precipitated a turning point in my life.

Remember that I did not *choose* any of these words in any of these poems in order to be cute or clever or comprehensive. These words seemed to pour out of me into the pen and onto the paper. Although I write prose often and at length, I have never tried to write another poem since that time in 1995. "Beyond Joy" was both my feeling at the time and the legal name of one of the peace pilgrims who walked from Auschwitz to Hiroshima. He is the subject of the next poem!

"The Land of the Morning Calm" has been used for many years by travel agents and other poets to describe all of Korea, North and South, because in the early morning the weather is almost always tranquil and often misty, even amidst their "purple mountain majesties."

Now you know why I entitled my reverie, "Be Calmed in Korea."

Please read it again before you meet my friends in Hiroshima.

Be Calmed in Korea

If you want peace,   be calm.
Calmness.   Peace.
Travel light,   for the journey is short.
Cash and carry.

It was after darkness fell,
as black as faith.
Lanterns lit, they led us out of town,
out of our control.

We wanted peace.   We were calm.
It was a good night.   Irene.
We arrived at dawn.   Beyond Joy.
The Land of the Morning Calm.

In early December of 1994, a very diverse group of about 200 potential peace pilgrims began their walk toward Hiroshima, departing from Poland at the site of the most infamous of Nazi concentration camps, Auschwitz. They were organized and led by Buddhist monks of the Nipponzan Myohoji Order. This Peace Walk traversed many countries, almost all of which had been devastated by warfare after World War II (since 1945). The pilgrims averaged twenty miles per day, and were kept going through the spiritual practice of walking, beating a prayer drum and chanting. Eight months later they arrived in Hiroshima, having covered well over 4000 miles. One hundred members of the original group were able to complete the entire journey.

Beyond Joy

That was his name. I kid you not.
He was a throwback to the 1960s.
Tall. Long blond hair. Quiet.
He wore a floppy black hat. Like Ray Bolger's Scarecrow?

He walked from Auschwitz to Hiroshima.
I kid you not. Try it sometime?
Beyond Joy.

When he arrived, the Japanese children knew who he was,
even though no words were spoken.
A deck of cards appeared. They played Concentration.
I watched them out of the corner of my eye.

I don't think he tried to win the game,
but he did win......them.

Joel

Joel also walked from Auschwitz to Hiroshima.
He said Cambodia was the best country, the Least Western.

An artillery shell landed in their compound one night,
but it didn't explode.
Joel got food poisoning and parasites,
but he made it.

While the other 99 finished the Peace Walk in Hiroshima,

Joel stayed behind and cleaned up after them.
He even scrubbed the kitchen floor,
for God's sake.

Beyond Joy and Joel were among those who made it to Japan, to be joined by 50,000 others in Hiroshima for the 50th commemoration of the atomic bombing. This included a group of U. S. Veterans for Peace who had been led by Korean Buddhist monks on a Peace Walk of 25 miles, northward from Seoul to the DMZ that still separates South Korea from North Korea. I was in that smaller contingent of peace pilgrims.

Robert and Marianne

From Chicago. Totally blind.
Never been out of the country.
Robert hit the road walking in Bosnia
and he never looked back.

Marianne had closed up her shoppe in Paris
and turned her eye to the Rising Sun.
Marianne truly was a woman of the world,
and like Lily in a Bob Dylan song,
there was a certain kind of a flash
every time she smiled.

In Hiroshima, mon amour,
she and he said that the beach
in Thailand had been fantastic.
And now? She said New Zealand sounds great.

Penny

Her name back home in Germany was Renate.
She changed it to Penny for the Peace Walk
so more people in more countries

could pronounce it and remember it.

Like me, Penny was no spring chicken,
and, like me, she had a bad knee.
The first day in Bosnia, they walked 28 clicks
on snow and ice,
two steps forward and one back.
Note that, you Vietnam veterans.

In Hiroshima, while the others packed up for Nagasaki,
Penny cleaned the toilets and raked the yard.
She told me where you could still eat cheaply in Japan
and where the best museums and castles were.

Once a German...always a German.

I should mention that "Lily" appears in Dylan's "most fun"
song, "Lily, Rosemary and the Jack of Hearts." *Hiroshima, Mon
Amour* is a French film from the 1950s. Penny and I were both
"going like sixty" in 1995. A "click" is soldier talk for a
kilometer; 28 clicks would be about 17 miles. Many of the
military veterans in the group that started at Auschwitz did not
complete the Peace Walk; some had flashbacks of Vietnam
when in jungle surroundings. And the line "...always a
German"... I resemble that remark!

Maea

His name is pronounced "my–ah" and it's spelled m–a–e–a...
and he is an indigenous person from an island near Chile.
Very good-looking, his hair a bit wild, Maea spoke English well
and clearly,
maybe better than most of us ... because there were no wasted
words.

Maea was part of "The Sacred Run" for 1995,
when native people from all over the earth ran 1400 miles

from the northern tip of Hokkaido to the southern tip of
Kyushu.
On one stretch between Hiroshima and Nagasaki they ran for 35
hours without stopping.

All Maea needed to live, including a good camera, was in one
bag.
I envied him.
How many people do we meet who are really free?

Naoko

She was eighteen and had postponed her last year of high school
in Tokyo
so she could walk from Auschwitz to Hiroshima.

She had reached her destination
when I met her on a crowded subway train
with Maea from Chile, Anna from Poland and Ariel from New
Hampshire.

Her journey had resulted in some nasty insect bites on her legs,
but to say her face was merely beautiful is a disservice to
reality.

I asked for her name......now, how do words on a page
communicate to you what I heard?
As she spoke, I heard the soft tones of wind-chimes
high on a windy hill.
She whispered, "My name is Naoko... Na–o–ko...
it means *gentle speaker*."

In 1996 "The Sacred Run" traversed the United States,
from Los Angeles, California to the site of the Olympic Games
in Atlanta, Georgia. Several weeks after being at the 1995
Hiroshima events, Ariel Brugger from New Hampshire walked
from our house in Minnesota to Washington, D.C. Traveling

mostly alone, she stopped in many cities and towns along the way to speak against the use of land mines and cluster bombs. During the earlier Peace Walk she had seen the devastation caused by those cruel anti-personnel weapons against the civilian populations of countries in Southeast Asia.

Hiroko

There is a Zen Buddhist saying,
"When the pupil is ready, the teacher will appear."

After I arrived in Japan, I phoned my home in Minnesota
and my wife asked me to do two things …
First, to go to the Hiroshima Peace Park
and take a picture of the sculpture of Sadako,
the girl who tried to fold 1000 paper cranes
before she died of radiation poisoning;
And then to pray for a friend of ours
who was starting her treatments for cancer.
I was more than willing to make that connection.

Later, as I approached the Sadako memorial site,
I noticed a young Japanese woman
finishing a watercolor painting of the sculpture.
I asked for her name and if I could take a picture of her,
her painting and the Sadako statue.
Hiroko smiled and complied.
Then I asked where she went to school.
Hiroko smiled and replied,
"I am the teacher."

Yes you are, Hiroko.
"When the pupil is ready, the teacher will appear."

In August of 1945, U.S. President Harry Truman, under considerable pressure from the Pentagon, gave the green light to drop the only two atomic bombs in existence to obliterate Hiroshima and Nagasaki, causing hundreds of thousands of civilians to die then or later. Before Truman gave that approval, he relied on a report from a group of twelve men who had prepared the plans for a late 1945 invasion of Japan. One of those men was my uncle, George Kemmer, an expert on the topography of Japan, especially its coastlines. Those twelve men were responsible for the estimate that an invasion of the two main islands of Japan might result in one million Allied casualties (dead and wounded) in the initial stages of such a sea-to-land invasion. For this reason, many people believe that the atomic bombing of Japan was justified, or even necessary. However, the full reality of the situation was quite different: Japan was a defeated nation before the bombs were dropped, and the decision had already been made to get out of the war, to seek a peace negotiation within two to three weeks at most. (Cf. the monograph *Japan's Struggle to End the War* by John Kenneth Galbraith)

The moral questions about all of this remain. Carolyn Forché, a well-known and talented American poet, has written a book-length poem called *The Angel of History*, in which she encourages us, "If you are still able to cry, you should go to Hiroshima." I returned to Korea and then went to Hiroshima in 1995 to make some personal amends, but also to represent an international movement, Veterans For Peace, and to give voice to its motto: **Abolish War**. In my poems I have portrayed a small number of peace messengers and some of the ways they spoke their truth to the powers of this world.

. The other 50,000 peace pilgrims who were with us then in Japan had their own reasons and made their own statements, but we were of one spirit as we fasted and prayed all day in the hot sun at the Hiroshima Peace Park on the 6th of August 1995.

Roy Wolfe has worked since 1985 in the Twin Cities as a Peace Education Coordinator offering workshops, seminars, retreats and courses on peace and social justice topics. His course, Six Stages of Personal Peacemaking, has been offered throughout Minnesota. The course was the basis for his book *Many Are Called, but Most Are Frozen: A Guide for Hawks, Doves and Ostriches*. In 1980 he helped create the Peace Studies Task Force, a grassroots response to the reestablishment of registration for military draft. As a member of Veterans for Peace since 1985, his aim is to abolish war by nonviolent peacemaking.

Lynne Zotalis

What Is Your Truth?

Flying back from Mexico with my husband's body entombed in the cargo hold, I grip the armrests as if I'm hanging onto sanity. "Not here next year" presses into my thoughts, beckoning from an echo chamber, swirling like a vortex. Vaguely familiar, I can barely make it out. It's calling from another dimension, a shock wave pulling me down, away from reality. There's music, a beautifully ethereal melody speaking to my psyche. I recognize it: Thomas Otten's "Qualitati Umane." Someone, something is drawing me away.

Chuck, is that you? Where are you, my love? Blinding iridescence hinders my sight as I search the luminous clouds. I can sense you just beyond reach. Are you out there? I can't get any air. Instinctively, I double over gasping for breath, contractions tying my stomach into a knot. You're twenty feet below me, your body in a casket. I can't breathe. I cup both hands over my mouth recalling those haunting words, "What if we're not here next year?"

Come on. Hang on. You have to keep it together. A few more hours and I'll see the kids, our four adult children for the heart wrenching reunion. With my eyes tightly shut, I try to envision it. Are you speaking to me? I sit upright, inhaling deeply as if in labor. My tenuous grip on reality vacillates floating in and out of subconsciousness.

Did I expect any other response phoning my folks from Mexico? It was a trial run before I attempted to break the news to our children.

"Hello," Edith said.

"Mom," I could barely get it out.

"Lynne? What's wrong? What happened?"

"Sit down," then I blurted, "Chuck died."

"What? Chuck? How?"

The other extension clicked. Dad said, "What's going on?"

Edith told him. Then the third click. My sister, Cynthia was visiting them, "What's the matter? Who?"

Peppered with questions, crying, I could give no understanding. Not willing to waste any more precious minutes with the salvo, I pitched the impossible, "I need money, Dad."

Zip. He took on businessman mode, clearing his throat, "Oh..., well..., what are you talking, how much?"

"I need $10,000 to make this happen. I have to have ready capital for persuasion, to work this system and buy my way out, if necessary. I need help."

Edith interjected, "We don't have that kind of money sitting around. We're not made of money."

"Ahhhhgg," I groaned, feeling my stomach knot.

Even now, I had to beg. I had no energy to argue or convince. Their refusal was the cruelest blow.

Slightly conciliatory, Dad said, "I'll have to see what I can come up with. It will take some time, juggling some things around."

"Forget it. Don't bother," I spewed, hating them.

*"Well, now, don't be like that. We'll see what we can do, "
Edith offered.*

*"I have to go. I have to call the kids. Goodbye, " I snapped,
icily, sinking down, down, down into panic.*

*When I called them several hours, later my sister and Dad
tried to explain the prudence of charging me the current interest
rate on whatever monies sent. Stunned by such a callous
contingency I refused the repugnant offer.*

*I told myself, "I will get through this without you,
goddammit! I don't need you. And I will never ask you again. "*

*Each shattering call back to the states compounded my
pain as I delivered the brutal death blow. Holding Chuck's
lifeless head in my hands was something I had no control over,
but now, saying the words, hurting my kids, was a conscious act
I took direct responsibility for:*

"Alexis, I have some horrible news.

She said nothing.

"Are you sitting down? " I stammered.

*There was no way to soften it. I had to crush her heart,
over the telephone, from Mexico.*

"Dad died. "

She implored softly, "Mom... what? What happened? "

*I tried to keep my voice coherent, level, giving her the
information I had.*

*Realizing Chuck's mom had to be told, I added, "You have
to go over and tell Grandma. I can't tell her on the phone, she
won't be able to comprehend it. I'm so sorry, honey, I'm so
sorry.... "*

Reflecting back, certain early memories made the most
profound impression based on my parents' response and my
level of pain. Others were fleeting frames projected against my
subconscious: mercurochrome painted adhesive taped fingers to
cure my forbidden sucking habit; a blackened jacket, filthy from
sliding down the steeply pitched coal dust coated driveway;

paper dolls balanced against the riser, their demise irreversible as the staircase crevices swallowed them up.

My earliest recollection was imprinted from a bicycle accident. Sitting on the thick metal rear fender, legs dangling in the cool breeze, arms clenched around my babysitter's waist, a jolt ripped my tender flesh to the bone as we jerked to a halt. Searing pain pierced my twisted ankle as it tangled through bike spokes. She carried me home howling, screaming for help. It took weeks for the swelling to subside, purple and blue to return pink. The emotional trauma healed much more slowly than my battered foot. Miraculously, no bones were broken.

"No, I don't want a bike!"

It was my chronic answer whenever my Depression-era parents, Jack and Edith, asked what I wanted for my birthday. I wanted a tractor like my grandpa had, like the one I showed Mommy from the catalogue. Two wheelers resurrected the dreaded experience.

Jack and Edith led me to the front door, "Open your eyes."

There it was, sitting on the walkway, in all its shiny red glory: my brand-new miniature riding tractor. It was my fifth birthday and I was so unaccustomed to getting what I asked for, the second daughter of a hard-working pharmaceutical salesman-father and overwrought housewife-mother that I thought, "This is a dream." Wondrously, unexpectedly, it appeared. It was the best day of my life.

They gave in, even though my mother continuously felt it her duty to remind me, "You think we're made of money? Money doesn't grow on trees; waste not, want not; there are children starving in China."

The recurring theme was meant to instill utility, a standard response to deny anything new. My chubby build resulted from guilt over the unfinished plateful that murdered Asian children who'd fare better if I were fat.

The watershed year, 1968; it felt like life began the year I graduated from high school. Drifting apart over the past years,

my longtime friend Cheryl and I'd dreamed of our groovy
excursion since eighth grade. She had relatives in San
Francisco, me in Los Angeles, so we set our course and escaped
parental control for a month. From the bland Midwest to sunny,
happenin' Cal, we were flying to another planet. My L.A.
cousin, several years older, let me drive his royal blue Corvette
Stingray. Holy shit. Content to just sit behind the wheel, I was
completely freaked I'd wreck it, if given the opportunity. His
approbation convinced me to give it a shot. After many trial
runs back and forth on his side street, I was ready to "head out
on the highway, looking for adventure." God, I couldn't believe
it; driving his 'Vette! Well, trying to. Having extreme difficulty
with the tight clutch, I killed it at every stoplight. My
destination was Riverside Park where the hippies hung out. I
wanted them to see how cool we were driving a Corvette. What
took place was the complete opposite.

The flower-child epoch was in full swing on the West
Coast. As the park came into view, the appearance of
beautifully free-spirited young people, their disdain of
materialism evident, was a stark contrast to my Barbie doll
persona. Sitting cross legged on the grass, passing a joint, they
looked so peaceful, eyes closed, swaying to guitar music, a harp
chiming in, another thumping bongo drums. Some sang, others
danced barefoot, in see through, madras print skirts, their long
hair flowing. Couples embraced, making out, right there on the
lawn, in front of everybody. Freedom. Love. Immediately
seduced, the scene resonated to my core with authentic
expression. During my junior and senior years, I'd dabbled in
marijuana, downers and speed, which was when Cheryl had
given me a wide berth, but hadn't yet been initiated into hard
core LSD and other hallucinogenic substances. Intrigued by
news reports of hippies, feeling the immensely appealing
rebellion, my attraction was solidified. Seeing them first hand I
was enmeshed, eager to jump right in. Not so much Cheryl, the
barometer of reason. If she'd had the same reaction as me, I
might never have come back from that trip, mentally and
physically. All I needed was the slightest encouragement, a

partner to bolster me, and I would have stayed in California. Much to my disappointment, unconvinced, and unimpressed, she didn't buy any of it. On the flight home, Cheryl and I *were* in agreement, however, concerning the upcoming school year.

"I'm not even into college," I bemoaned.

"Ya, like I am," she said, laughing.

"I only signed up for Normandale to get Jack and Edith off my case."

Cheryl asked, "What else would you do?"

"Work, I guess. I don't know. Go back out to Cal."

The seed had been planted. I felt hooked. Churning, stirring, the questions compounded. What was my life about? Who was I? What did I want to be? What was truth? Love? Reality? Purpose? Did anyone have answers? Where could I find meaning? I didn't know *who* I was but was sick of being her. It took the next school year for me to summon the courage and resolve to follow my inner voice.

A life changing wave had rushed into my spirit that day in California and I was finally ready to be swept out to sea. Needing to discover, to understand what the hippie movement was all about, I ventured in. My wardrobe blossomed with baggy bell-bottoms, tie-dyed shirts, and the ultimate declaration, free-flowing breasts. It empowered me to wear clothes that aligned me with certain people and, at the same time, made others stare in disgust. I wanted to freak everyone out. My soul was screaming, "screw you and all your middle class values." Finally…a depth of existence I could relate to.

Vacating my parents' house where I had to pretend to be straight became top priority. While they were away on vacation, I hauled my belongings to the one-bedroom apartment Lana shared with her sister. In a great old red brick building on 36th and Girard Avenue, it was my ticket to freedom. Bolstering my resolve, I planned to confront the 'rents upon their return.

I toyed with buttressing the living room with friends to buffer the encounter like my brilliant defensive move at 16. After I totaled Edith's car, again while they were on vacation, I had four of my friends sit with me in the living room as I confessed. It was drama but they didn't kill me on the spot. This time I intended to face them alone, like an adult.

"I have some news," I said trying to sound confident, calm, mature.

Bracing themselves, jumping to the worst conclusion, they asked, "What's going on?"

"I moved into an apartment with Lana. It's a two bedroom down on Girard. I'm working and have enough money saved up and I have all my stuff there."

Mom asked, "What about school?"

Not softening it, I blurted, "I'm not going anymore. It's not what I want to do."

"Well, then what are you going to do?"

"I'm not sure. I have been doing a lot of thinking and I need to figure things out."

"Figure what out?" Dad asked, raising his voice in exasperation.

"Life."

"So exactly when do you think you're leaving?" Mom asked.

"Tonight," I said, belligerently.

"We can't let you do that."

"I'm eighteen. It's my right. You can't stop me. That's the fact. I'm going."

So I drove my car, Dad following in his, to inspect my new place. Giving it the once over, trying to intimidate me, *and* Lana, he tried to act like the decision was his.

Standing at the door, waiting for some weakening, something that would give him the excuse to demand obedience, sarcastically he said, "Well, good luck, I hope you find your answers," adding, "You know you've broken your mother's heart."

I stood, defiant; not wanting it to be like this but couldn't see any other way out. I had to get away from them.

Heaping it on, he finished with, "This will kill your mother."

Guilt is the gift that keeps on giving, and I could forever count on that generous dose. And guess what? She still lived! It was a miracle.

It was a movement I exuberantly jumped into over my head that summer in Minneapolis. 1969. Hundreds of 18-, 19-, and 20-year olds marching to the beat of unrest. Peace rallies and stoned out sit-ins at the U, the West Bank were standard fare, chanting the mantra, "make love, not war." The charged atmosphere encompassed the Vietnam War, unlimited sex, drugs, and rock and roll. I loved hanging out in the shared apartment, walking to Electric Fetus, Psychedelia, head shops. Lana and Linda shared the bedroom, so I took the couch. Fine, glorious, beautiful. Life was superb.

My heap of a car having tanked, I hitchhiked, alone, all over the city, fearlessly flaunting my liberation. Released from my inhibitions, bouncing braless, hair disheveled, clothes hanging off the shoulder, I had that "just raped" appearance. My one rule when sizing up a ride was: if the car was full of guys, I emphatically declared, no thanks. Relatively safe, it was just a way of life. I was only propositioned once, by an older man who mistook me for a hooker.

It was a kind of innocent bubble in some ways, a slice out of time like no other for those couple of years before the guns, the gangs, and the violence invaded our world. Music was mellow, ethereal or acid rockin', lyrics transporting us above and beyond the questions. The songs were a cultural phenomenon blasting our eardrums with the message of our generation. I didn't understand the wisdom of guides for acid trips, anything of that controlled nature. Totally unorthodox, we dangerously experimented with all the psychedelic drugs available. With the indestructible nescience of youth, I happened upon truth, reality and honesty by accident. Teetering on the precipice of insanity, the environment had to be carefully orchestrated or a bad trip could send one over the edge. That was the perilous instability about being high: hallucinations displacing reality with paranoia lurking dangerously close. You could keep control if the circle was tightly buttressed with those you trusted, the precarious balance maintained but admittedly, danger was a large part of the attraction, blending elements of bravado with unbelievable ignorance. By sheer coincidence, between the fun and excitement, enlightenment was unfolding.

Jeff, our best friend, fresh from the jungles of Vietnam, was trying to figure out what just happened to his life. Our crowd spent hours together rapping, playing albums, watching the visuals on T.V. He evolved from the physically and emotionally shattered vet to an anti-war freak like us, hating the government, the establishment, turning on and tuning out. Quiet, brooding, angry, and broken-hearted, Jeff unfolded over several months his ordeal, slowly verbalizing the details as he was able, reinforcing and educating us as to the immorality and horror of the war. How any young man in his early 20s could still function normally after what he'd been through was phenomenal. Wounded so severely, Jeff was the only soldier in the amputee ward who lucked out and kept all his limbs.

Jeff related the saga this way: *"After having already set up two positions of a blocking force on the riverside, eight of us were left to complete the final one. There was a sweep going on by the South Vietnamese, the ARVN, (Army of the Republic of Vietnam) supposedly, our allies. We understood the enemy, the Vietcong, to be on the opposite side, but they'd already crossed over. Walking into this clearing, we surprised twelve of them standing there. We gave chase as some dropped their weapons and fled. The radio man with my unit received reconnaissance from the helicopter overhead informing us that the enemy was running unarmed into the wood line.*

I said, "Let's go get 'em."

The troop's response was unanimous. As we stepped into the wood line, my watch broke falling off my wrist. In the second I bent down to pick it up and put it into my pocket, the machine gun fire ripped past me. Immediately, 15 feet to my left there was screaming. One of my guys was laying face down in about 18 inches of water. Stepping into the clearing, I was hit.

Blown back, slamming down, my weapon flew into the mango swamp. Frantically searching, I took a grenade and threw it, hitting a Nipa palm 15 feet away, the shrapnel narrowly missing my head. Dropping down completely under water for cover, I realized how badly I was hit. I could hear air sucking through the holes in my body. Every time I tried to get to my man, they'd drop the barrel down right at the surface, skipping bullets across to finish me off. I had to back away, leaving him there, his head partially exposed, brains sticking out. He was dead. I was sure of it. The helicopter, a scout, came within view. They motioned me to go this one direction. I was kinda walking, getting up, stumbling, up, down, stumbling, up, then down. I got about 50 meters. The chopper dropped down but the water was too deep. They motioned me in another direction. Somehow I made it to where they could recover me. The gunner scrambled out to help me and this memory is so vivid: when he jumped out running, he'd forgotten to take his helmet off, all attached with the wires so his head jerks backwards, yanking him down. The humor wasn't lost on me, even under those gruesome circumstances. He got me into the chopper, and as we lifted up, I'm in the back, all by myself, looking up, looking around, observing a few of my guys, and everything goes bright red. Bright red. Blood. I passed out.

In the aide station, the first time I regained consciousness, dozens of people were rushing around. Nurses, doctors, medics. It was seconds, then I passed out again. The next time I came to, there was no one there.

I thought to myself, I fuckin' died. It ain't that bad. It didn't hurt that much.

But I was in a morphine haze. When I woke up the next time I was lucid enough to comprehend what was going on. The brigade commander, the battalion commander, brigade XO, and the battalion XO were all in the same helicopter, which is a huge no-no. You couldn't have that many command people in one helicopter. On their way into the base, a loaded gunship was heading out when they collided, killing thirteen people, including all the command staff, all the pilots, even people on the ground. That accounted for all of the activity at the aide station. They shipped me by helicopter to the 3rd field hospital at Saigon. Trying to equalize the blood loss, my arm and shoulder had been tightly packed while two blood bags were continually pumped into me. Wheeling me to the x-ray unit, losing his grip amidst all the gore, the gurney aid dropped my arm letting it flop backwards, straight down at a 45-degree angle four inches above the elbow.

I screamed in agony, "You mother-fucker!"

This female nurse, a colonel, pulled up short, remarking, "You can't talk to us that way."

I shot back, "Oh, fuck you. I'll talk to you any goddam way I please. It's my arm you fuckin' dropped!"

Aside from that particular incident, they actually treated me pretty well. The first surgery at TanSonNhut air base aide station was a stopgap procedure that enabled me to hold enough blood to survive the transport to Japan. I had two more surgeries in 30 days wondering every minute whether I'd keep my limb. It was a mess, with the radial nerve severed.

Doctors of one opinion said, "Yank it."

Others, on my side, were saying, "It's not infected. It could just be traumatized. We need to give it more time."

My orthopedic surgeon was adamant, "There's no point in taking it yet."

He won.

A guy lying across from me, after having lost part of one leg, a little below the knee, didn't get his dressing changed for an entire day. In their defense, it was a horrible place for the medics to function, but through their neglect, gangrene set in. They had to keep chopping more and more off. Both legs were mid-thigh length by the time he was released. He started out missing part of a leg but because of that one day, both legs were amputated.

Another six months at the Kansas military base hospital got me to the discharge point."

I couldn't believe the lack of bitterness in Jeff. Deeply, profoundly wounded and shell-shocked, he retained his soft heart. It took him a long time to express the horror of that experience. Instead of talking, for months he chose to be alone with his thoughts trying to sort through the madness. Solidified in our anti-war stance, Jeff's ordeal reinforced our intention of running to Canada if our friend Chuck was drafted. The records were either destroyed or damaged when the draft office was bombed that year in Minneapolis. We were ecstatic. Chuck drew a high number when the lottery was instituted meaning it was very unlikely he'd be called. We breathed a sigh of relief but still kept a wary eye convinced of the lying government's corruption.

Nixon's adamant avowal, "I am not a crook!" was ludicrous.

God, how we hated him.

In a constant state of transition, my mind swirled as the hallucinogenic haze fueled doubt and suspicion of the status quo. During all night rap sessions, we espoused hip gurus; Kahlil Gibran, Herman Hesse, and Timothy Leary advising us to tune in, turn on and drop out. They made perfect sense, helping us sort life out with convincing revelations and logical arguments. I bought into the cultural phenomena of the *Whole Earth Catalog*, the *Foxfire* book, *The Book of the Hopi*, and *Black Elk Speaks*, formulating a radical way of life, with a dismissive attitude toward all my past values. High on acid, I could figure out all of my problems....until the deflation the next day when I came down. The answer was simple: remain in the altered state.

Over the next few months, Chuck and I became confidantes. Our respective romantic relationships were problematic. His girlfriend didn't dig the hippie direction he was heading in, and my current partner's behavior was suspect, at best, overtly distant and unfaithful at worst. I knew it wasn't cool to question his infidelities so I poured my heart out to

Chuck. Free love was the norm; relationships weren't often exclusive so to be bummed out about a myriad of sleeping partners was not hip. But it wasn't ever that simple. Home alone, trying to adopt the appearance of nonchalance, I'd pour my heart out writing into the wee hours. Being friends with Chuck, platonically, was unique. Without the sexual component in the equation, the relaxed atmosphere as we rapped, hanging out, smoking dope was refreshingly uncomplicated. Our tight bond of friendship developed as we empathized.

"I was slated to go into the Air Force," Chuck told me one night, sitting in his apartment.

"Really?! I can't imagine why you'd be into that. Isn't that the last place you'd want to be?"

"Ya, well, before I got into drugs and got my shit together, I was pretty right wing. That all changed in the last year. Anyway, they flew me to Michigan for the whole Air Force orientation. I was pretty impressed with the pilots walking around base in their flight suits. They're on such huge ego trips. I went through the physical, the testing, and passed everything."

"So what changed your mind?"

"I found out I could fly without planes!" Chuck said, cracking up.

But then the mood shifting drastically, he continued, "I've had ten friends come home in body bags. I was in a guy's wedding in the spring and went to his funeral a few months later. Ten from my high school class!"

This is where it got real. Our generation shipped off to an illegal war. Hearing our friend Jeff relate his experience, actually seeing the destruction to his body, and understanding the disillusionment in his psyche—too real.

Becoming connected to Chuck in heart and soul forged a bond. We were searching for truth, seeking ways to change the current culture. "Back to the land" was the vision Chuck and I embraced, resolving to escape from society's military machine. We'd fed the dream continually over the last couple years espousing and reinforcing the themes of country life, nature, and anti-establishment. Our honeymoon was a road trip to the mountains of New Mexico where dozens of hippies, fulfilling the dream, cemented our life's goal to move there, build a log cabin, and abide happily ever after in peace. Already having friends from Minneapolis, Ed and Dominique, living in New Mexico lent credence to our plan. We idolized those brave, convention-thwarting pioneers, figuring we had as much chutzpa.

The 'rents' didn't buy it for a second.

"We'll live off the land," we said, trying to explain the pathway of perfection to Jack.

"Are you crazy?" Edith asked, adding, "That's the dumbest thing I ever heard."

"What're you going to do for money? What about jobs? What do you mean, living off the land?" Their questions flew at us in rapid fire.

"We'll figure something out. We're going to save up before we head out there. It'll work," we vainly argued with both sets of 'rents.

Wonderful, simple, idealistic youth!

Snow-frosted peaks and majestic spruce set against a backdrop of salmon and rust layered canyons aptly depicted the "Land of Enchantment." The bewitching atmosphere in northern New Mexico at 8,000 feet and the grandeur took our breath away. Kept alive by native peoples, the rich spiritual history lent intoxicating mystery to our environment. Surrounded by pristine beauty, this manifestation of love power joined with the philosophy of flower children took root in one of the most extraordinary places on earth. The Mesa was another world, a new beginning. The year was 1972. Like-minded families escaped the draft, political unrest, and unbridled right-wing hatred to find Shangri-La in a sparsely populated area whose indigenous residents traced their land titles to the 1600s, some having deeds signed by the King of Spain.

What a shock to be nine miles from the nearest store, post office box, and telephone. Ed helped us locate the plot of land we needed to make our dream a reality. A clear title was so nebulous, so rare on the Mesa that the "hips"—we Anglos—submitted to the law of the land. In a method resembling squatter's rights, we obtained permission to build our cabin. Two feuding Spanish factions, brothers Rogelio, Nestor and Samuel in contention with their cousin Tony as to rightful possession, claimed ownership to "our" piece of property.

"We just want to live here," we innocently proffered, propositioning the opposing family members as we talked to them about our desire to build a log cabin on the plot in question, "What's the hassle?"

I loved the American Indian belief about land possession; we are one with the earth. Not having a title, just simply borrowing the land, was a concept we could embrace.

Securing approval wasn't difficult. The cousins knew Ed, who vouched for us. We were friendly, naive, harmless looking city folks. Going to each feuding member's house, in turn with a case of beer in hand, Chuck and I nodded in agreement with the cousins, promising allegiance to both sides of the family, and swearing loyalty to gain their permission. We had a deal.

We set up camp with an ancient cook stove that presented no easy task learning its quirks. I burned everything before painstakingly mastering the particular balance of fuel regulation. Our borrowed tent housed belongings and supplies; Chuck and I snuggled together during the cool nights. A crystal clear creek running year round provided us with drinking water. The multifarious families on the Mesa were our lifeblood; not a commune but a community, joined by camaraderie of intention. We identified with an altruistic dream of working toward the possibility of a socialist ideal. The vision we believed not attainable in middle class America was pursued by those bound in a common purpose to live in peace and harmony with nature and mankind, using only what was necessary.

Our disappointed parents waited, hoping for a conciliatory letter or a white flag of surrender. Through the pay phone at the general store we kept in contact with them about once a week. Faithfully, I wrote, but my timbre was arrogant, boasting of our progress. Chuck's folks drove across country to see us before much had been accomplished on our cabin. They were horrified! Their only child had gone to college for this!? After showing them the "grounds," we drove to Santa Fe for a profoundly strained visit. I thought it wiser not to announce my pregnancy just yet.

For two years, having birthed Alexis in the log cabin, Chuck and I clung tenaciously to Thoreau's admonition, "Go confidently in the direction of your dreams. Live the life you have imagined." Ebulliently, Chuck and I had expected all of our problems to disappear when we disentangled ourselves from city existence. Many of the hippies, after abandoning dreams of a perfect society in neighboring communes, had sought a new beginning on the Mesa. Now, faced with glaring discrepancies between theory and practice, sensing the dawn of dissolution, our search for peace took a dramatic turn. The feeling was one of understanding, a reckoning. Was it a voice, a premonition, a spiritual insight? We'd never be able to explain it, but were totally mystified by the abrupt awakening, the sense that the chapter had ended.

"We can live here, alone," Chuck reasoned, explaining his thoughts, "but how can we raise Alexis here? How will I make a living and provide for what she needs? This isn't fair to her or to you."

Our conversation went well into the night, as we stoked the potbellied stove, hashing over details. Neither of us wanted to bail out, but didn't see any way to sustain our life in the mountains with no way to meet our financial needs. It broke our hearts to leave, but maturity comes at a cost. With trepidation we resolved to go back to Minnesota, concluding that the ideal, the dream wasn't geographically realized. It came from within, deep within one's soul.

I took his hands across the table as my tears spilled out, "It's you and me, Babe. Whatever we do, wherever we go, we'll figure it out. Together. That's all that really matters."

Raising his hands to my face, I kissed his fingers one by one.

"I love you," he whispered.

When I'd pitched the Mexican vacation to Chuck, I admitted, "I know it'll be a stretch, but we've always denied ourselves everything. Isn't it time to be crazy, impractical? Isn't it time for us? It's our thirtieth anniversary. We have to do something big. What if we're not here next year?"

He didn't say anything, just sat there pondering. The wheels were in motion and I understood his need for space. This was how it worked with us. If I pushed, he'd dig in his heels. His method of always looking at situations more slowly as he weighed every detail had taught me patience. In the early years I would get so frustrated feeling like I was being ignored, but after thirty years, I had figured it out; plant a seed, zip it, and wait. Over dinner a couple nights later, when I brought up the Mexican vacation, he laid his fork down, giving me one of his penetrating looks. Reaching across the table, he took my hand.

I loved his affection, his smile, as he squeezed tenderly, "You're right, we need to do this."

It's been 14 years since Chuck died, 40 since we lived on the Mesa and rarely a day passes that I'm not reminded in some way of both. I maintain relationships with those friends having a life enriched by our experiences in the '70s. The passage of time _is_ ultimately the miraculous healer. Alexis, then 26, told the people at Chuck's memorial service: "My dad taught me these important tenets. Life is not fair, and be thankful for what you have."

I admit I am a work in progress, still pursuing the intrinsic conviction to _be_ a peacemaker. Where does it get fleshed out? In our everyday existence. In our home life. Are we living in peace and love? If our family can't witness it in our lives, we need to ask why. I didn't haul my children to peace demonstrations when they were young. It just wasn't possible. But what I could do was show them an act of generosity, simply. On any outing upon seeing a homeless person, I would drive to the nearest fast food restaurant, purchase a meal, throw any change in the bag, drive back and hand over the food. Without fanfare or much explanation, the object lesson came across. Thirty years later my daughter told me how that impacted her.

The vision Chuck and I sought and shared from the first, at that anti-war rally in 1969, cemented a conviction spanning the rest of our lives. Some truths have evolved through the years such as motives my parents may have had raising me. I've come to be extremely grateful for the strength of character they instilled in me. Witnessing their marriage that was rife with conflict and animosity, I swore never to have a relationship resembling theirs; rather, I would strive for a life with peace, love and truth. That was my choice and I was fortunate enough to find a partner who believed likewise.

My relationship with Chuck—our heart and soul connection—remained vibrant through three decades raising our four children. We were always mindful to cherish our rare private moments. These elements are woven forever through the tapestry of my life.

This is my truth.

Lynne Zotalis   Despite having lived in Decorah, Iowa, for fifteen years, I still identify myself as a Minnesotan by birth and decades of residence. The mother of four adult children and three grandchildren, my work included floral design and a lifelong writing avocation. My publication, *Saying Goodbye to Chuck*, available on amazon.com, was written as a journaling tool to assist those suffering from the loss of a loved one. To find peace and hope, enable healing and to move forward is the book's purpose.

As a member in the Loft Literary Center's Peace and Social Justice Writers Group in Minneapolis, I am privileged to be involved with talented and productive individuals promoting hope and well-being. Two of my writings were included in the chapbook entitled *Peace Begins* published by the group and available on www.lulu.com. I was interviewed by John Noltner for his book, *A Peace of my Mind*, a Midwest book award winner; the podcast of the same can be heard at: http://www.apeaceofmymind.net .

I'm a member in the Iowa Poetry Association and my poems have appeared in *Lyrical Iowa* and my essays in the local magazine, *Inspire(d)* www.theinspiredmedia.com.

For the past two years, I have been involved with Winneshiek County Protectors, winneshiekcountyprotectors.com. Our goal is to safeguard Northeast Iowa from the impact of large-scale mining of silica sand. It is imperative we employ wise management of our valuable natural resources, carefully and expeditiously ensuring a future for the generations to come. I truly believe we can make a difference as demonstrated so admirably by one of Decorah's finest examples: Bob Anderson, recently deceased Director of the Raptor Resource Project, and longtime resident who restored the peregrine falcon population with his unflinching efforts. We take heart in such success, to live a life of Peaceful Acts and Conscious Thought—PACT.

Afterword

Walk into The Open Book complex of transformed industrial buildings from busy Washington Avenue in downtown Minneapolis. Groups of writers are at work around café tables. The Minnesota Center for Book Arts celebrates the book as a vibrant contemporary art form in workshop and gallery areas. A gently winding staircase lined with panels of writing ascends to meeting spaces, classrooms, an auditorium, and the offices of the Loft Literary Center.

Founded in 1974 (incorporated in 1975), the Loft Literary Center is one of the nation's leading literary arts centers. The Loft advances the artistic development of writers, fosters a thriving literary community, and inspires a passion for literature. Our core values are that literature is essential, writing can be taught, inclusiveness is imperative, boldness brings excellence, community makes us strong, and wise management fuels our success.

Since its foundation, the Loft has welcomed writers of color, indigenous writers, and writers who identify with the LGBTQ community with varied programming and events. Programs and events, such as the Mentor Series, Equilibrium (EQ), and Talking Volumes, still operate today and work to create a more representative and diverse literary landscape in the Twin Cities and nationwide. Past programs and projects such as the Inroads Program, Sunday Slams, and the Loft-McKnight International Residency program, to name just a few, have made significant impacts in terms of community and diversity.

One such initiative is the Loft's Open Groups. These are self-selecting and largely self-governed cohorts of writers and include the Peace and Social Justice Writers Group, one of the longest tenured groups, whose work you hold in your hands right now.

The Peace and Social Justice writers do nothing less than explore the nature of peace. Emphasizing the intersections and collisions of writing, social justice, and equity, the hardworking members of this group have gathered for years to share their work and provoke vital conversations. They have welcomed new members, and their rotating leaders have brought different perspectives and strengths to the fold. These activists and writers recognize the potential for effective critical discourse inherent in the medium of writing and its potential to be a catalyst for change. Poet Michael Kiesow Moore's class at The Loft (Writing Peace Into Your Life) was the foundation for the group's formation.

In addition to their monthly meetings, the Peace and Social Justice Writers also organize readings and other events. They were seminal in facilitating the designation of the Open Book building as an International Peace Site in 2015. At the ceremony, the Peace and Social Justice group welcomed participants from other writing groups such as the TGI Frybread Native American Writers Group and the Equilibrium spoken word program.

As the Loft Literary Center moves into the future, we plan to continue focusing on writing, social justice, and equity. We're grateful to the Peace and Social Justice Writers Group for their important contributions to our community, and congratulate them on their part in the publication of this volume. May our words and work move us all ever closer to a more peaceful and just world.

Bao Phi, Program Director
The Loft Literary Center

Acknowledgments

Working on a collection of essays cross-country (and cross-ocean) has been an electronic adventure. All participants acknowledge the challenges involved, the patience required as well as the fun and sense of discovery that has been a part of this project. But it's the vision that counts. Laurence Peters had the vision which sparked participation and enthusiasm. Burt Berlowe brought that spark to the Peace and Social Justice Writers Group and to other contributors. Many thanks go to those who participated as essay writers and to others who contributed by listening and sharing their comments and suggestions. Thanks also to Philip Lund as the P&SJ group's moderator and to Shea Hansen for her empowering insights.

A big thank you to California activist and writer Karin Pally for her comments and editorial work. The role of The Loft Literary Center in providing a supportive and friendly space for writers to meet is warmly acknowledged.

A special thanks to Christina Kieltyka for her art work "The Memory Tree" that appears on the cover. And thanks also to Samantha Fernandez for her work on the cover design.

ChangingTimesPress
ChangingTimesPress.com